# The Complete Salter Air Fryer Cookbook UK

*Quick, Easy and Healthy Recipes for Your Salter Air Fryer with European Measurement& Ingredients*

**<u>Tilly Doherty</u>**

**All Rights Reserved.**

**Notice Of Disclaimer.**

# CONTENTS

# Beef , pork & Lamb Recipes ................................................................. 33

# Vegetarians Recipes ...................................................... 72

# TIPS FOR AIR FRYER SUCCESS

## Know Your Appliance

First, and most important, read your appliance manual. All air fryers are not created equal. Features differ among models. Even timers work differently. Parts of some air fryers may be dishwasher safe, but you may have to hand-wash others. Any misuse of your air fryer or its parts could void the warranty. Read all safety information, and never use the machine in any way that violates the manufacturer's instructions for safe use. In addition to keeping you safe, your manual should provide details about your model's features and functions. Most of us hate reading instructions or manuals, but it's worth taking the time to understand how to use it. Sometimes that can make all the difference between frustration and success.

## Cooking Time

Many factors can affect cooking times, including size, volume, and temperature of food, thickness of breading, and so on. Even your local humidity levels can affect required cooking times. Wattage is another factor. All recipes in this cookbook were tested in 1,425-watt air fryers. A unit with a higher or lower wattage may cook somewhat faster or slower. For most recipes, total cooking time shouldn't vary by more than a minute or two, but to avoid overcooking, check food early and often. Always start with the shortest cooking time listed in a recipe. Check for doneness at that point and continue cooking if necessary. When you try a recipe for the first time and the minimum cooking time is, say, 20 minutes or longer, check the dish at about 15 minutes just to be safe. If you're new to air frying, don't be afraid to pause your air fryer often to open the drawer and check foods. That's the best way to save dinner before it overcooks or burns.

# Minimum Temperatures for Food Safety

Consuming raw or undercooked eggs, fish, game, meats, poultry, seafood, or shellfish may increase your risk of foodborne illness. To ensure that foods are safe to eat, ground beef, lamb, pork, and veal should be cooked to a minimum of 75°C/160°F. Other cuts of these meats such as beef steaks should be cooked to at least 65°C/145°F. All turkey and chicken should be cooked to a minimum of 75°C/165°F.

Cooking in Batches

For best results, always cut foods into uniform pieces so they cook more evenly. Follow recipes to know whether foods can be stacked or must cook in a single layer. Directions will indicate whether you need to turn or shake the basket to redistribute foods during cooking. All recipes developed for this cookbook were tested in air fryers with an interior capacity of approximately 3 quarts. Using these "standard"-size air fryers often requires cooking in two batches, but many foods cook so quickly that this additional cooking time doesn't matter.

For foods that require lengthy cooking time, the first batch may cool too much while the second batch is cooking, but the solution is simple. Air fryers do an excellent job of reheating foods. Right before your second batch finishes cooking, place your first batch on top so it reheats for serving. If there's not enough room in your air fryer basket, wait until the second batch is done, remove it, and reheat the first batch for a minute or two. Keep this strategy in mind any time you need to heat up leftovers. They come out hot and crispy—unlike microwave-reheated foods, which can feel soggy, rubbery, or tough.

You can also buy a larger air fryer. Some models have a capacity of approximately 5 quarts. If you have an air fryer of this size, you may be able to cook many of our recipes in a single batch. Follow recipe instructions as to whether a particular food can be crowded or stacked, and fill the basket accordingly. You may need to adjust recipe times slightly, but after cooking a few recipes, you'll know how to judge that.

# Smoking

Select a suitable location for your unit. If possible, place it near your range so you can use the vent hood if needed. Follow the manufacturer's instructions to protect your countertop and to allow the required amount of open space around the back, sides, and top of your air fryer. Smoking isn't a frequent problem but does occur when cooking meats or other foods with a high fat content. Adding water to the air fryer drawer can help sometimes but not always. Coconut, for example, tends to smoke no matter what. An accumulation of grease in the bottom of your air fryer can also cause smoking. Prevent this problem by keeping the drawer clean and free of food or fat buildup.

Excessive smoking, especially black smoke, is not normal. This could result from an electrical malfunction, in which case unplug your appliance immediately and contact the manufacturer.

# Appetizers And Snacks Recipes

## Fried Brie With Cherry Tomatoes

Servings: 8
Cooking Time: 15 Minutes
**Ingredients:**

- 1 baguette*
- 2 pints red and yellow cherry tomatoes
- 1 tablespoon olive oil
- salt and freshly ground black pepper
- 1 teaspoon balsamic vinegar
- 1 tablespoon chopped fresh parsley
- 1 (8-ounce) wheel of Brie cheese
- olive oil
- ½ teaspoon Italian seasoning (optional)
- 1 tablespoon chopped fresh basil

**Directions:**

1. Preheat the air fryer to 350°F.
2. Start by making the crostini. Slice the baguette diagonally into ½-inch slices and brush the slices with olive oil on both sides. Air-fry the baguette slices at 350°F in batches for 6 minutes or until lightly browned on all sides. Set the bread aside on your serving platter.
3. Toss the cherry tomatoes in a bowl with the olive oil, salt and pepper. Air-fry the cherry tomatoes for 3 to 5 minutes, shaking the basket a few times during the cooking process. The tomatoes should be soft and some of them will burst open. Toss the warm tomatoes with the balsamic vinegar and fresh parsley and set aside.
4. Cut a circle of parchment paper the same size as your wheel of Brie cheese. Brush both sides of the Brie wheel with olive oil and sprinkle with Italian seasoning, if using. Place the circle of parchment paper on one side of the Brie and transfer the Brie to the air fryer basket, parchment side down. Air-fry at 350°F for 8 to 10 minutes, or until the Brie is slightly puffed and soft to the touch.
5. Watch carefully and remove the Brie before the rind cracks and the cheese starts to leak out. Transfer the wheel to your serving platter and top with the roasted tomatoes. Sprinkle with basil and serve with the toasted bread slices.

## Crunchy Pickle Chips

Servings: 4

Cooking Time: 20 Minutes
**Ingredients:**

- 1 lb dill pickles, sliced
- 2 eggs
- 1/3 cup flour
- 1/3 cup bread crumbs
- 1 tsp Italian seasoning

**Directions:**

1. Preheat air fryer to 400°F. Set out three small bowls. In the first bowl, add flour. In the second bowl, beat eggs. In the third bowl, mix bread crumbs with Italian seasoning. Dip the pickle slices in the flour. Shake, then dredge in egg. Roll in bread crumbs and shake excess. Place the pickles in the greased frying basket and Air Fry for 6 minutes. Flip them halfway through cooking and fry for another 3 minutes until crispy. Serve warm.

## Smoked Whitefish Spread

Servings: 1
Cooking Time: 10 Minutes
**Ingredients:**

- ¾ pound Boneless skinless white-flesh fish fillets, such as hake or trout
- 3 tablespoons Liquid smoke
- 3 tablespoons Regular, low-fat, or fat-free mayonnaise (gluten-free, if a concern)
- 2 teaspoons Jarred prepared white horseradish (optional)
- ¼ teaspoon Onion powder
- ¼ teaspoon Celery seeds
- ¼ teaspoon Table salt
- ¼ teaspoon Ground black pepper

**Directions:**

1. Put the fish fillets in a zip-closed bag, add the liquid smoke, and seal closed. Rub the liquid smoke all over the fish , then refrigerate the sealed bag for 2 hours.
2. Preheat the air fryer to 400°F.
3. Set a 12-inch piece of aluminum foil on your work surface. Remove the fish fillets from the bag and set them in the center of this piece of foil (the fillets can overlap). Fold the long sides of the foil together and crimp them closed.

Make a tight seam so no steam can escape. Fold up the ends and crimp to seal well.

4. Set the packet in the basket and air-fry undisturbed for 10 minutes.

5. Use kitchen tongs to transfer the foil packet to a wire rack. Cool for a minute or so. Open the packet, transfer the fish to a plate, and refrigerate for 30 minutes.

6. Put the cold fish in a food processor. Add the mayonnaise, horseradish (if using), onion powder, celery seeds, salt, and pepper. Cover and pulse to a slightly coarse spread, certainly not fully smooth.

7. For a more traditional texture, put the fish fillets in a bowl, add the other ingredients, and stir with a wooden spoon, mashing the fish with everything else to make a coarse paste.

8. Scrape the spread into a bowl and serve at once, or cover with plastic wrap and store in the fridge for up to 4 days.

# Spinach Cups

Servings: 30
Cooking Time: 5 Minutes
**Ingredients:**

- 1 6-ounce can crabmeat, drained to yield ⅓ cup meat
- ¼ cup frozen spinach, thawed, drained, and chopped
- 1 clove garlic, minced
- ½ cup grated Parmesan cheese
- 3 tablespoons plain yogurt
- ¼ teaspoon lemon juice
- ½ teaspoon Worcestershire sauce
- 30 mini phyllo shells (2 boxes of 15 each), thawed
- cooking spray

**Directions:**

1. Remove any bits of shell that might remain in the crabmeat.

2. Mix crabmeat, spinach, garlic, and cheese together.

3. Stir in the yogurt, lemon juice, and Worcestershire sauce and mix well.

4. Spoon a teaspoon of filling into each phyllo shell.

5. Spray air fryer basket and arrange half the shells in the basket.

6. Cook at 390°F for 5minutes.

7. Repeat with remaining shells.

# Tasty Serrano Tots

Servings:4
Cooking Time: 30 Minutes
**Ingredients:**

- ¾ cup riced cauliflower
- 2 serrano peppers, minced
- 1 egg
- 1/3 cup grated sharp cheddar
- 1 oz cream cheese, softened
- 1 tbsp onion powder
- 1/3 cup flour
- ½ tsp salt
- ¼ tsp garlic powder

**Directions:**

1. Preheat air fryer to 375°F. Mix the riced cauliflower, serrano peppers, egg, cheddar, cream cheese, onion, flour, salt, and garlic powder in a bowl. Form into 12 rectangular mounds. Add the tots to the foil-lined frying basket and Air Fry for 8-10 minutes. Let chill for 5 minutes before serving. Enjoy!

# Thai-style Crabwontons

Servings: 4
Cooking Time: 20 Minutes
**Ingredients:**

- 4 oz cottage cheese, softened
- 2 ½ oz lump crabmeat
- 2 scallions, chopped
- 2 garlic cloves, minced
- 2 tsp tamari sauce
- 12 wonton wrappers
- 1 egg white, beaten
- 5 tbsp Thai sweet chili sauce

**Directions:**

1. Using a fork, mix together cottage cheese, crabmeat, scallions, garlic, and tamari sauce in a bowl. Set it near your workspace along with a small bowl of water. Place one wonton wrapper on a clean surface. The points should be facing so that it looks like a diamond. Put 1 level tbsp of the crab and cheese mix onto the center of the wonton wrapper. Dip your finger into the water and run the moist finger along the edges of the wrapper.

2. Fold one corner of the wrapper to the opposite side and make a triangle. From the center out, press out any air and seal the edges. Continue this process until all of the wontons have been filled and sealed. Brush both sides of the wontons with beaten egg white.

3. Preheat air fryer to 340°F. Place the wontons on the bottom of the greased frying basket in a single layer. Bake for 8 minutes, flipping the wontons once until golden brown and crispy. Serve hot and enjoy!

## Chipotle Sunflower Seeds

Servings:4
Cooking Time: 20 Minutes
**Ingredients:**
- 2 cups sunflower seeds
- 2 tsp olive oil
- ½ tsp chipotle powder
- 1 garlic clove, minced
- ¼ tsp salt
- 1 tsp granulated sugar

**Directions:**

1. Preheat air fryer to 325ºF. In a bowl, mix the sunflower seeds, olive oil, chipotle powder, garlic, salt, and sugar until well coated. Place the mixture in the frying basket and Air Fry for 10 minutes, shaking once. Serve chilled.

## Polenta Fries With Chili-lime Mayo

Servings: 4
Cooking Time: 28 Minutes
**Ingredients:**
- 2 teaspoons vegetable or olive oil
- ¼ teaspoon paprika
- 1 pound prepared polenta, cut into 3-inch x ½-inch sticks
- salt and freshly ground black pepper
- Chili-Lime Mayo
- ½ cup mayonnaise
- 1 teaspoon chili powder
- ¼ teaspoon ground cumin
- juice of half a lime
- 1 teaspoon chopped fresh cilantro

- salt and freshly ground black pepper

**Directions:**
1. Preheat the air fryer to 400°F.
2. Combine the oil and paprika and then carefully toss the polenta sticks in the mixture.
3. Air-fry the polenta fries at 400°F for 15 minutes. Gently shake the basket to rotate the fries and continue to air-fry for another 13 minutes or until the fries have browned nicely. Season to taste with salt and freshly ground black pepper.
4. To make the chili-lime mayo, combine all the ingredients in a small bowl and stir well.
5. Serve the polenta fries warm with chili-lime mayo on the side for dipping.

## Bbq Chips

Servings: 2
Cooking Time: 30 Minutes
**Ingredients:**
- 1 scrubbed russet potato, sliced
- ½ tsp smoked paprika
- ¼ tsp chili powder
- ¼ tsp garlic powder
- 1/8 tsp onion powder
- ¼ tbsp smoked paprika
- 1/8 tsp light brown sugar
- Salt and pepper to taste
- 2 tsp olive oil

**Directions:**
1. Preheat air fryer at 400ºF. Combine all seasoning in a bowl. Set aside. In another bowl, mix potato chips, olive oil, black pepper, and salt until coated. Place potato chips in the frying basket and Air Fry for 17 minutes, shaking 3 times. Transfer it into a bowl. Sprinkle with the bbq mixture and let sit for 15 minutes. Serve immediately.

16

# Crunchy Parmesan Edamame

Servings:4
Cooking Time: 25 Minutes + Cooling Time
**Ingredients:**

- 1 cup edamame, shelled
- 1 tbsp sesame oil
- 1 tsp five-spice powder
- ½ tsp salt
- ½ tsp garlic powder
- ¼ cup grated Parmesan

**Directions:**
1. Cook the edamame in boiling salted water until crisp-tender, about 10 minutes. Drain and leave to cool. Preheat air fryer to 350°F. Combine edamame, garlic, and sesame oil in a bowl. Place them in the frying basket and Air Fry for 16 minutes, shaking twice. Transfer to a small bowl and toss with five-spice powder and salt. Serve chilled topped with Parmesan cheese. Enjoy!

# Fried String Beans With Greek Sauce

Servings: 4
Cooking Time: 10 Minutes
**Ingredients:**

- 1 egg
- 1 tbsp flour
- ¼ tsp paprika
- ½ tsp garlic powder
- Salt to taste
- ¼ cup bread crumbs
- ¼ lemon zest
- ½ lb whole string beans
- ½ cup Greek yogurt
- 1 tbsp lemon juice
- ⅛ tsp cayenne pepper

**Directions:**
1. Preheat air fryer to 380°F. Whisk the egg and 2 tbsp of water in a bowl until frothy. Sift the flour, paprika, garlic powder, and salt in another bowl, then stir in the bread crumbs. Dip each string bean into the egg mixture, then roll into the bread crumb mixture. Put the string beans in a single layer in the greased frying basket. Air Fry them for 5 minutes until the breading is golden brown. Stir the yogurt, lemon juice and zest, salt, and cayenne in a small bowl. Serve the bean fries with lemon-yogurt sauce.

# Curried Pickle Chips

Servings: 4
Cooking Time: 25 Minutes
**Ingredients:**

- 2 dill pickles, sliced
- 1 cup breadcrumbs
- 2 eggs, beaten
- A pinch of white pepper
- 1 tsp curry powder
- ½ tsp mustard powder

**Directions:**
1. Preheat air fryer to 350°F. Combine the breadcrumbs, curry, mustard powder, and white pepper in a mixing bowl. Coat the pickle slices with the crumb mixture; then dip into the eggs, then dip again into the dry ingredients. Arrange the coated pickle pieces on the greased frying basket in an even layer. Air Fry for 15 minutes, shaking the basket several times during cooking until crispy, golden brown and perfect. Serve warm.

# Hot Cauliflower Bites

Servings: 4
Cooking Time: 35 Minutes
**Ingredients:**

- 1 head cauliflower, cut into florets
- 1 cup all-purpose flour
- 1 tsp garlic powder
- 1/3 cup cayenne sauce

**Directions:**
1. Preheat air fryer to 370°F. Mix the flour, 1 cup of water, and garlic powder in a large bowl until a batter forms. Coat cauliflower in the batter, then transfer to a large bowl to drain excess. Place the cauliflower in the greased frying basket without stacking. Spray with cooking, then Bake for 6 minutes. Remove from the air fryer and transfer to a large

17

bowl. Top with cayenne sauce. Return to the fryer and cook for 6 minutes or until crispy. Serve.

## Avocado Fries With Quick Salsa Fresca

Servings: 4
Cooking Time: 6 Minutes
**Ingredients:**

- ½ cup flour*
- 2 teaspoons salt
- 2 eggs, lightly beaten
- 1 cup panko breadcrumbs*
- ⅛ teaspoon cayenne pepper
- ¼ teaspoon smoked paprika (optional)
- 2 large avocados, just ripe
- vegetable oil, in a spray bottle
- Quick Salsa Fresca
- 1 cup cherry tomatoes
- 1 tablespoon-sized chunk of shallot or red onion
- 2 teaspoons fresh lime juice
- 1 teaspoon chopped fresh cilantro or parsley
- salt and freshly ground black pepper

**Directions:**
1. Set up a dredging station with three shallow dishes. Place the flour and salt in the first shallow dish. Place the eggs into the second dish. Combine the breadcrumbs, cayenne pepper and paprika (if using) in the third dish.
2. Preheat the air fryer to 400°F.
3. Cut the avocado in half around the pit and separate the two sides. Slice the avocados into long strips while still in their skin. Run a spoon around the slices, separating them from the avocado skin. Try to keep the slices whole, but don't worry if they break – you can still coat and air-fry the pieces.
4. Coat the avocado slices by dredging them first in the flour, then the egg and then the breadcrumbs, pressing the crumbs on gently with your hands. Set the coated avocado fries on a tray and spray them on all sides with vegetable oil.
5. Air-fry the avocado fries, one layer at a time, at 400°F for 6 minutes, turning them over halfway through the cooking time and spraying lightly again if necessary. When the fries are nicely browned on all sides, season with salt and remove.

6. While the avocado fries are air-frying, make the salsa fresca by combining everything in a food processor. Pulse several times until the salsa is a chunky purée. Serve the fries warm with the salsa on the side for dipping.

## Caponata Salsa

Servings: 6
Cooking Time: 16 Minutes
**Ingredients:**

- 4 cups (one 1-pound eggplant) Purple Italian eggplant(s), stemmed and diced (no need to peel)
- Olive oil spray
- 1½ cups Celery, thinly sliced
- 16 (about ½ pound) Cherry or grape tomatoes, halved
- 1 tablespoon Drained and rinsed capers, chopped
- Up to 1 tablespoon Minced fresh rosemary leaves
- 1½ tablespoons Red wine vinegar
- 1½ teaspoons Granulated white sugar
- ¾ teaspoon Table salt
- ¾ teaspoon Ground black pepper

**Directions:**
1. Preheat the air fryer to 350°F .
2. Put the eggplant pieces in a bowl and generously coat them with olive oil spray. Toss and stir, spray again, and toss some more, until the pieces are glistening.
3. When the machine is at temperature, pour the eggplant pieces into the basket and spread them out into an even layer. Air-fry for 8 minutes, tossing and rearranging the pieces twice.
4. Meanwhile, put the celery and tomatoes in the same bowl the eggplant pieces had been in. Generously coat them with olive oil spray; then toss well, spray again, and toss some more, until the vegetables are well coated.
5. When the eggplant has cooked for 8 minutes, pour the celery and tomatoes on top in the basket. Air-fry undisturbed for 8 minutes more, until the tomatoes have begun to soften.
6. Pour the contents of the basket back into the same bowl. Add the capers, rosemary, vinegar, sugar, salt, and pepper. Toss well to blend, breaking up the tomatoes a bit to create more moisture in the mixture.
7. Cover and refrigerate for 2 hours to blend the flavors. Serve chilled or at room temperature. The caponata salsa can stay in its covered bowl in the fridge for up to 2 days before the vegetables weep too much moisture and the dish becomes too wet.

# Cheesy Spinach Dip(1)

Servings: 6
Cooking Time: 35 Minutes
**Ingredients:**

- ½ can refrigerated breadstick dough
- 8 oz feta cheese, cubed
- ¼ cup sour cream
- ½ cup baby spinach
- ½ cup grated Swiss cheese
- 2 green onions, chopped
- 2 tbsp melted butter
- 4 tsp grated Parmesan cheese

**Directions:**

1. Preheat air fryer to 320°F. Blend together feta, sour cream, spinach, Swiss cheese, and green onions in a bowl. Spread into the pan and Bake until hot, about 8 minutes. Unroll six of the breadsticks and cut in half crosswise to make 12 pieces. Carefully stretch each piece and tie into a loose knot. Tuck in the ends to prevent burning.

2. When the dip is ready, remove the pan from the air fryer and place each bread knot on top of the dip until the dip is covered. Brush melted butter on each knot and sprinkle with Parmesan. Bake until the knots are golden, 8-13 minutes. Serve warm.

# Tasty Roasted Black Olives & Tomatoes

Servings: 6
Cooking Time: 25 Minutes
**Ingredients:**

- 2 cups grape tomatoes
- 4 garlic cloves, chopped
- ½ red onion, chopped
- 1 cup black olives
- 1 cup green olives
- 1 tbsp thyme, minced
- 1 tbsp oregano, minced
- 2 tbsp olive oil
- ½ tsp salt

**Directions:**

1. Preheat air fryer to 380°F. Add all ingredients to a bowl and toss well to coat. Pour the mixture into the frying basket and Roast for 10 minutes. Stir the mixture, then Roast for an additional 10 minutes. Serve and enjoy!

# Antipasto-stuffed Cherry Tomatoes

Servings: 12
Cooking Time: 9 Minutes
**Ingredients:**

- 12 Large cherry tomatoes, preferably Campari tomatoes (about 1½ ounces each and the size of golf balls)
- ½ cup Seasoned Italian-style dried bread crumbs (gluten-free, if a concern)
- ¼ cup (about ¾ ounce) Finely grated Parmesan cheese
- ¼ cup Finely chopped pitted black olives
- ¼ cup Finely chopped marinated artichoke hearts
- 2 tablespoons Marinade from the artichokes
- 4 Sun-dried tomatoes (dry, not packed in oil), finely chopped
- Olive oil spray

**Directions:**

1. Preheat the air fryer to 400°F.
2. Cut the top off of each fresh tomato, exposing the seeds and pulp. (The tops can be saved for a snack, sprinkled with some kosher salt, to tide you over while the stuffed tomatoes cook.) Cut a very small slice off the bottom of each tomato (no cutting into the pulp) so it will stand up flat on your work surface. Use a melon baller to remove and discard the seeds and pulp from each tomato.
3. Mix the bread crumbs, cheese, olives, artichoke hearts, marinade, and sun-dried tomatoes in a bowl until well combined. Stuff this mixture into each prepared tomato, about 1½ tablespoons in each. Generously coat the tops of the tomatoes with olive oil spray.
4. Set the tomatoes stuffing side up in the basket. Air-fry undisturbed for 9 minutes, or until the stuffing has browned a bit and the tomatoes are blistered in places.
5. Remove the basket and cool the tomatoes in it for 5 minutes. Then use kitchen tongs to gently transfer the tomatoes to a serving platter.

# Italian-style Fried Olives

Servings: 4
Cooking Time: 25 Minutes
**Ingredients:**

- 1 jar pitted green olives
- ½ cup all-purpose flour
- Salt and pepper to taste
- 1 tsp Italian seasoning
- ½ cup bread crumbs
- 1 egg

**Directions:**

1. Preheat air fryer to 400°F. Set out three small bowls. In the first, mix flour, Italian seasoning, salt and pepper. In the bowl, beat the egg. In the third bowl, add bread crumbs. Dip the olives in the flour, then the egg, then in the crumbs. When all of the olives are breaded, place them in the greased frying basket and Air Fry for 6 minutes. Turn them and cook for another 2 minutes or until brown and crispy. Serve chilled.

# Middle Eastern Phyllo Rolls

Servings: 6
Cooking Time: 5 Minutes
**Ingredients:**

- 6 ounces Lean ground beef or ground lamb
- 3 tablespoons Sliced almonds
- 1 tablespoon Chutney (any variety), finely chopped
- ¼ teaspoon Ground cinnamon
- ¼ teaspoon Ground coriander
- ¼ teaspoon Ground cumin
- ¼ teaspoon Ground dried turmeric
- ¼ teaspoon Table salt
- ¼ teaspoon Ground black pepper
- 6 18 × 14-inch phyllo sheets (thawed, if necessary)
- Olive oil spray

**Directions:**

1. Set a medium skillet over medium heat for a minute or two, then crumble in the ground meat. Cook for 3 minutes, stirring often, or until well browned. Stir in the almonds, chutney, cinnamon, coriander, cumin, turmeric, salt, and pepper until well combined. Remove from the heat, scrape the cooked ground meat mixture into a bowl, and cool for 15 minutes.

2. Preheat the air fryer to 400°F.

3. Place one sheet of phyllo dough on a clean, dry work surface. (Keep the others covered.) Lightly coat it with olive oil spray, then fold it in half by bringing the short ends together. Place about 3 tablespoons of the ground meat mixture along one of the longer edges, then fold both of the shorter sides of the dough up and over the meat to partially enclose it (and become a border along the sheet of dough). Roll the dough closed, coat it with olive oil spray on all sides, and set it aside seam side down. Repeat this filling and spraying process with the remaining phyllo sheets.

4. Set the rolls seam side down in the basket in one layer with some air space between them. Air-fry undisturbed for 5 minutes, or until very crisp and golden brown.

5. Use kitchen tongs to transfer the rolls to a wire rack. Cool for only 2 or 3 minutes before serving hot.

# Cayenne-spiced Roasted Pecans

Servings: 4
Cooking Time: 15 Minutes
**Ingredients:**

- ¼ tsp chili powder
- Salt and pepper to taste
- ⅛ tsp cayenne pepper
- 1 tsp cumin powder
- 1 tsp cinnamon powder
- ⅛ tsp garlic powder
- ⅛ tsp onion powder
- 1 cup raw pecans
- 2 tbsp butter, melted
- 1 tsp honey

**Directions:**

1. Preheat air fryer to 300°F. Whisk together black pepper, chili powder, salt, cayenne pepper, cumin, garlic powder, cinnamon, and onion powder. Set to the side. Toss pecans, butter, and honey in a medium bowl, then toss in the spice mixture. Pour pecans in the frying basket and toast for 3 minutes. Stir the pecans and toast for another 3 to 5 minutes until the nuts are crisp. Cool and serve.

# Cinnamon Apple Crisps

Servings: 1
Cooking Time: 22 Minutes
**Ingredients:**

- 1 large apple
- ½ teaspoon ground cinnamon
- 2 teaspoons avocado oil or coconut oil

**Directions:**

1. Preheat the air fryer to 300°F.
2. Using a mandolin or knife, slice the apples to ¼-inch thickness. Pat the apples dry with a paper towel or kitchen cloth. Sprinkle the apple slices with ground cinnamon. Spray or drizzle the oil over the top of the apple slices and toss to coat.
3. Place the apple slices in the air fryer basket. To allow for even cooking, don't overlap the slices; cook in batches if necessary.
4. Cook for 20 minutes, shaking the basket every 5 minutes. After 20 minutes, increase the air fryer temperature to 330°F and cook another 2 minutes, shaking the basket every 30 seconds. Remove the apples from the basket before they get too dark.
5. Spread the chips out onto paper towels to cool completely, at least 5 minutes. Repeat with the remaining apple slices until they're all cooked.

# Sweet Potato Chips

Servings: 4
Cooking Time: 10 Minutes
**Ingredients:**

- 2 medium sweet potatoes, washed
- 2 cups filtered water
- 1 tablespoon avocado oil
- 2 teaspoons brown sugar
- ½ teaspoon salt

**Directions:**

1. Using a mandolin, slice the potatoes into ⅛-inch pieces.
2. Add the water to a large bowl. Place the potatoes in the bowl, and soak for at least 30 minutes.
3. Preheat the air fryer to 350°F.
4. Drain the water and pat the chips dry with a paper towel or kitchen cloth. Toss the chips with the avocado oil, brown sugar, and salt. Liberally spray the air fryer basket with olive oil mist.
5. Set the chips inside the air fryer, separating them so they're not on top of each other. Cook for 5 minutes, shake the basket, and cook another 5 minutes, or until browned.
6. Remove and let cool a few minutes prior to serving. Repeat until all the chips are cooked.

# Zucchini Fritters

Servings: 8
Cooking Time: 10 Minutes
**Ingredients:**

- 2 cups grated zucchini
- ½ teaspoon sea salt
- 1 egg
- ½ teaspoon garlic powder
- ¼ teaspoon onion powder
- ¼ cup grated Parmesan cheese
- ½ cup all-purpose flour
- ¼ teaspoon baking powder
- ½ cup Greek yogurt or sour cream
- ½ lime, juiced
- ¼ cup chopped cilantro
- ¼ teaspoon ground cumin
- ¼ teaspoon salt

**Directions:**

1. Preheat the air fryer to 360°F.
2. In a large colander, place a kitchen towel. Inside the towel, place the grated zucchini and sprinkle the sea salt over the top. Let the zucchini sit for 5 minutes; then, using the towel, squeeze dry the zucchini.
3. In a medium bowl, mix together the egg, garlic powder, onion powder, Parmesan cheese, flour, and baking powder. Add in the grated zucchini, and stir until completely combined.
4. Pierce a piece of parchment paper with a fork 4 to 6 times. Place the parchment paper into the air fryer basket. Using a tablespoon, place 6 to 8 heaping tablespoons of fritter batter onto the parchment paper. Spray the fritters with cooking spray and cook for 5 minutes, turn the fritters over, and cook another 5 minutes.
5. Meanwhile, while the fritters are cooking, make the sauce. In a small bowl, whisk together the Greek yogurt or sour cream, lime juice, cilantro, cumin, and salt.

6. Repeat Steps 2–4 with the remaining batter.

# Chinese-style Potstickers

Servings: 6
Cooking Time: 30 Minutes
**Ingredients:**

- 1 cup shredded Chinese cabbage
- ¼ cup chopped shiitake mushrooms
- ¼ cup grated carrots
- 2 tbsp minced chives
- 2 garlic cloves, minced
- 2 tsp grated fresh ginger
- 12 dumpling wrappers
- 2 tsp sesame oil

**Directions:**

1. Preheat air fryer to 370°F. Toss the Chinese cabbage, shiitake mushrooms, carrots, chives, garlic, and ginger in a baking pan and stir. Place the pan in the fryer and Bake for 3-6 minutes. Put a dumpling wrapper on a clean workspace, then top with a tablespoon of the veggie mix.

2. Fold the wrapper in half to form a half-circle and use water to seal the edges. Repeat with remaining wrappers and filling. Brush the potstickers with sesame oil and arrange them on the frying basket. Air Fry for 5 minutes until the bottoms should are golden brown. Take the pan out, add 1 tbsp of water, and put it back in the fryer to Air Fry for 4-6 minutes longer. Serve hot.

# Buffalo Wings

Servings: 2
Cooking Time: 12 Minutes Per Batch
**Ingredients:**

- 2 pounds chicken wings
- 3 tablespoons butter, melted
- ¼ cup hot sauce (like Crystal® or Frank's®)
- Finishing Sauce:
- 3 tablespoons butter, melted
- ¼ cup hot sauce (like Crystal® or Frank's®)
- 1 teaspoon Worcestershire sauce

**Directions:**

1. Prepare the chicken wings by cutting off the wing tips and discarding (or freezing for chicken stock). Divide the drumettes from the wingettes by cutting through the joint. Place the chicken wing pieces in a large bowl.

2. Combine the melted butter and the hot sauce and stir to blend well. Pour the marinade over the chicken wings, cover and let the wings marinate for 2 hours or up to overnight in the refrigerator.

3. Preheat the air fryer to 400°F.

4. Air-fry the wings in two batches for 10 minutes per batch, shaking the basket halfway through the cooking process. When both batches are done, toss all the wings back into the basket for another 2 minutes to heat through and finish cooking.

5. While the wings are air-frying, combine the remaining 3 tablespoons of butter, ¼ cup of hot sauce and the Worcestershire sauce. Remove the wings from the air fryer, toss them in the finishing sauce and serve with some cooling blue cheese dip and celery sticks.

# Charred Shishito Peppers

Servings: 4
Cooking Time: 5 Minutes
**Ingredients:**

- 20 shishito peppers (about 6 ounces)
- 1 teaspoon vegetable oil
- coarse sea salt
- 1 lemon

**Directions:**

1. Preheat the air fryer to 390°F.

2. Toss the shishito peppers with the oil and salt. You can do this in a bowl or directly in the air fryer basket.

3. Air-fry at 390°F for 5 minutes, shaking the basket once or twice while they cook.

4. Turn the charred peppers out into a bowl. Squeeze some lemon juice over the top and season with coarse sea salt. These should be served as finger foods – pick the pepper up by the stem and eat the whole pepper, seeds and all. Watch for that surprise spicy one!

# Spiced Roasted Pepitas

Servings:4
Cooking Time: 25 Minutes
**Ingredients:**

- 2 cups pumpkin seeds
- 1 tbsp butter, melted
- Salt and pepper to taste
- ½ tsp shallot powder
- ½ tsp smoked paprika
- ½ tsp dried parsley
- ½ tsp garlic powder
- ¼ tsp dried chives
- ¼ tsp dry mustard
- ¼ tsp celery seed

**Directions:**

1. Preheat air fryer to 325ºF. Combine the pumpkin seeds, butter, and salt in a bowl. Place the seed mixture in the frying basket and Roast for 13 minutes, turning once. Transfer to a medium serving bowl. Stir in shallot powder, paprika, parsley, garlic powder, chives, dry mustard, celery seed, and black pepper. Serve right away.

# Fried Wontons

Servings: 24
Cooking Time: 6 Minutes
**Ingredients:**

- 6 ounces Lean ground beef, pork, or turkey
- 1 tablespoon Regular or reduced-sodium soy sauce or tamari sauce
- 1½ teaspoons Minced garlic
- ¾ teaspoon Ground dried ginger
- ½ teaspoon Ground white pepper
- 24 Wonton wrappers (thawed, if necessary)
- Vegetable oil spray

**Directions:**

1. Preheat the air fryer to 350°F .
2. Stir the ground meat, soy or tamari sauce, garlic, ginger, and white pepper in a bowl until the spices are uniformly distributed in the mixture.
3. Set a small bowl of water on a clean, dry surface or next to a clean, dry cutting board. Set one wonton wrapper on the surface. Dip your clean finger in the water, then run it along the edges of the wrapper. Set 1 teaspoon of the ground meat mixture in the center of the wrapper. Fold it over, corner to corner, to create a filled triangle. Press to seal the edges, then pull the corners on the longest side up and together over the filling to create the classic wonton shape. Press the corners together to seal. Set aside and continue filling and making more filled wontons.
4. Generously coat the filled wontons on all sides with vegetable oil spray. Arrange them in the basket in one layer and air-fry for 6 minutes, shaking the basket gently at the 2- and 4-minute marks to rearrange the wontons (but always making sure they're still in one layer), until golden brown and crisp.
5. Pour the wontons in the basket onto a wire rack or even into a serving bowl. Cool for 2 or 3 minutes (but not much longer) and serve hot.

# Classic Chicken Wings

Servings: 8
Cooking Time: 20 Minutes
**Ingredients:**

- 16 chicken wings
- ¼ cup all-purpose flour
- ¼ teaspoon garlic powder
- ¼ teaspoon paprika
- ½ teaspoon salt
- ½ teaspoon black pepper
- ¼ cup butter
- ½ cup hot sauce
- ½ teaspoon Worcestershire sauce
- 2 ounces crumbled blue cheese, for garnish

**Directions:**

1. Preheat the air fryer to 380°F.
2. Pat the chicken wings dry with paper towels.
3. In a medium bowl, mix together the flour, garlic powder, paprika, salt, and pepper. Toss the chicken wings with the flour mixture, dusting off any excess.
4. Place the chicken wings in the air fryer basket, making sure that the chicken wings aren't touching. Cook the chicken wings for 10 minutes, turn over, and cook another 5 minutes. Raise the temperature to 400°F and continue crisping the chicken wings for an additional 3 to 5 minutes.
5. Meanwhile, in a microwave-safe bowl, melt the butter and hot sauce for 1 to 2 minutes in the microwave. Remove from the microwave and stir in the Worcestershire sauce.
6. When the chicken wings have cooked, immediately transfer the chicken wings into the hot sauce mixture. Serve the coated chicken wings on a plate, and top with crumbled blue cheese.

# Bread And Breakfast Recipes

## Avocado Toasts With Poached Eggs

Servings: 4
Cooking Time: 15 Minutes
Ingredients:

- 4 eggs
- Salt and pepper to taste
- 4 bread pieces, toasted
- 1 pitted avocado, sliced
- ½ tsp chili powder
- ½ tsp dried rosemary

Directions:

1. Preheat air fryer to 320°F. Crack 1 egg into each greased ramekin and season with salt and black pepper. Place the ramekins into the air frying basket. Bake for 6-8 minutes.
2. Scoop the flesh of the avocado into a small bowl. Season with salt, black pepper, chili powderp and rosemary. Using a fork, smash the avocado lightly. Spread the smashed avocado evenly over toasted bread slices. Remove the eggs from the air fryer and gently spoon one onto each slice of avocado toast. Serve and enjoy!

## Cajun Breakfast Potatoes

Servings: 4
Cooking Time: 20 Minutes
Ingredients:

- 1 pound roasting potatoes (like russet), scrubbed clean
- 1 tablespoon vegetable oil
- 2 teaspoons paprika
- ½ teaspoon garlic powder
- ¼ teaspoon onion powder
- ¼ teaspoon ground cumin
- 1 teaspoon thyme
- 1 teaspoon sea salt
- ½ teaspoon black pepper

Directions:

1. Cut the potatoes into 1-inch cubes.
2. In a large bowl, toss the cut potatoes with vegetable oil.
3. Sprinkle paprika, garlic powder, onion powder, cumin, thyme, salt, and pepper onto the potatoes, and toss to coat well.
4. Preheat the air fryer to 400°F for 4 minutes.
5. Add the potatoes to the air fryer basket and bake for 10 minutes. Stir or toss the potatoes and continue baking for an additional 5 minutes. Stir or toss again and continue baking for an additional 5 minutes or until the desired crispness is achieved.

## Spring Vegetable Omelet

Servings: 4
Cooking Time: 20 Minutes
Ingredients:

- ¼ cup chopped broccoli, lightly steamed
- ½ cup grated cheddar cheese
- 6 eggs
- ¼ cup steamed kale
- 1 green onion, chopped
- Salt and pepper to taste

Directions:

1. Preheat air fryer to 360°F. In a bowl, beat the eggs. Stir in kale, broccoli, green onion, and cheddar cheese. Transfer the mixture to a greased baking dish and Bake in the fryer for 15 minutes until golden and crisp. Season to taste and serve immediately.

## Morning Burrito

Servings: 4
Cooking Time: 15 Minutes
Ingredients:

- 2 oz cheddar cheese, torn into pieces
- 2 hard-boiled eggs, chopped
- 1 avocado, chopped
- 1 red bell pepper, chopped
- 3 tbsp salsa
- 4 flour tortillas

**Directions:**

1. Whisk the eggs, avocado, red bell pepper, salsa, and cheese. Pout the tortillas on a clean surface and divide the egg mix between them. Fold the edges and roll up; poke a toothpick through so they hold. Preheat air fryer to 390°F. Place the burritos in the frying basket and Air Fry for 3-5 minutes until crispy and golden. Serve hot.

**Directions:**

1. Preheat air fryer to 350°F. Mix the oats, apple, cherries, and cinnamon in a heatproof bowl. Add in milk and Bake for 6 minutes, stir well and Bake for 6 more minutes until the fruit are soft. Serve cooled.

## Banana-blackberry Muffins

Servings: 6
Cooking Time: 20 Minutes
**Ingredients:**

- 1 ripe banana, mashed
- ½ cup milk
- 1 tsp apple cider vinegar
- 1 tsp vanilla extract
- 2 tbsp ground flaxseed
- 2 tbsp coconut sugar
- ¾ cup flour
- 1 tsp baking powder
- ½ tsp baking soda
- ¾ cup blackberries

**Directions:**

1. Preheat air fryer to 350°F. Place the banana in a bowl. Stir in milk, apple vinegar, vanilla extract, flaxseed, and coconut sugar until combined. In another bowl, combine flour, baking powder, and baking soda. Pour it into the banana mixture and toss to combine. Divide the batter between 6 muffin molds and top each with blackberries, pressing slightly. Bake for 16 minutes until golden brown and a toothpick comes out clean. Serve cooled.

## Broccoli Cornbread

Servings: 6
Cooking Time: 18 Minutes
**Ingredients:**

- 1 cup frozen chopped broccoli, thawed and drained
- ¼ cup cottage cheese
- 1 egg, beaten
- 2 tablespoons minced onion
- 2 tablespoons melted butter
- ½ cup flour
- ½ cup yellow cornmeal
- 1 teaspoon baking powder
- ½ teaspoon salt
- ¼ cup milk, plus 2 tablespoons
- cooking spray

**Directions:**

1. Place thawed broccoli in colander and press with a spoon to squeeze out excess moisture.
2. Stir together all ingredients in a large bowl.
3. Spray 6 x 6-inch baking pan with cooking spray.
4. Spread batter in pan and cook at 330°F for 18 minutes or until cornbread is lightly browned and loaf starts to pull away from sides of pan.

## Cherry-apple Oatmeal Cups

Servings: 2
Cooking Time: 20 Minutes
**Ingredients:**

- 2/3 cup rolled oats
- 1 cored apple, diced
- 4 pitted cherries, diced
- ½ tsp ground cinnamon
- ¾ cup milk

## Orange Cran-bran Muffins

Servings: 4
Cooking Time: 30 Minutes
**Ingredients:**

- 1 ½ cups bran cereal flakes
- 1 cup flour
- 3 tbsp granulated sugar
- 1 tbsp orange zest
- 1 tsp baking powder

- 1 cup milk
- 3 tbsp peanut oil
- 1 egg
- ½ cup dried cranberries

**Directions:**

1. Preheat air fryer to 320°F. Combine the cereal, flour, granulated sugar, orange zest, and baking powder in a bowl, and in another bowl, beat the milk, oil, and egg. Add the egg mix to the dry ingredients and stir, then add the cranberries and stir again. Make 8 foil muffin cups by doubling 16 cups. Set 4 cups in the frying basket and spoon the batter in the cups until they're ¾ full. Bake for 15 minutes or until the tops bounce when touched. Set the muffins on a wire rack for 10 minutes, then serve.

# Walnut Pancake

Servings: 4
Cooking Time: 20 Minutes
**Ingredients:**

- 3 tablespoons butter, divided into thirds
- 1 cup flour
- 1½ teaspoons baking powder
- ¼ teaspoon salt
- 2 tablespoons sugar
- ¾ cup milk
- 1 egg, beaten
- 1 teaspoon pure vanilla extract
- ½ cup walnuts, roughly chopped
- maple syrup or fresh sliced fruit, for serving

**Directions:**

1. Place 1 tablespoon of the butter in air fryer baking pan. Cook at 330°F for 3minutes to melt.
2. In a small dish or pan, melt the remaining 2 tablespoons of butter either in the microwave or on the stove.
3. In a medium bowl, stir together the flour, baking powder, salt, and sugar. Add milk, beaten egg, the 2 tablespoons of melted butter, and vanilla. Stir until combined but do not beat. Batter may be slightly lumpy.
4. Pour batter over the melted butter in air fryer baking pan. Sprinkle nuts evenly over top.
5. Cook for 20minutes or until toothpick inserted in center comes out clean. Turn air fryer off, close the machine, and let pancake rest for 2minutes.

6. Remove pancake from pan, slice, and serve with syrup or fresh fruit.

# Lime Muffins

Servings: 6
Cooking Time: 30 Minutes
**Ingredients:**

- 1 ½ tbsp butter, softened
- 6 tbsp sugar
- 1 egg
- 1 egg white
- 1 tsp vanilla extract
- 1 tsp lime juice
- 1 lime, zested
- 5 oz Greek yogurt
- ¾ cup + 2 tbsp flour
- ¾ cup raspberries

**Directions:**

1. Beat butter and sugar in a mixer for 2 minutes at medium speed. In a separate bowl, whisk together the egg, egg white and vanilla. Pour into the mixer bowl, add lime juice and zest. Beat until combined. At a low speed, add yogurt then flour. Fold in the raspberries. Divide the mixture into 6 greased muffin cups using an ice cream scoop. The cups should be filled about ¾ of the way.
2. Preheat air fryer to 300°F. Put the muffins into the air fryer and Bake for 15 minutes until the tops are golden and a toothpick in the center comes out clean. Allow to cool before serving.

# Aromatic Mushroom Omelet

Servings: 4
Cooking Time: 30 Minutes
**Ingredients:**

- 6 eggs
- 2 tbsp milk
- ½ yellow onion, diced
- ½ cup diced mushrooms
- 2 tbsp chopped parsley
- 1 tsp dried oregano
- 1 tbsp chopped chives

- ½ tbsp chopped dill
- ½ cup grated Gruyère cheese

**Directions:**

1. Preheat air fryer to 350°F. Beat eggs in a medium bowl, then add the rest of the ingredients, except for the parsley. Stir until completely combined. Pour the mixture into a greased pan and bake in the air fryer for 18-20 minutes until the eggs are set. Top with parsley and serve.

# Wake-up Veggie & Ham Bake

Servings:4
Cooking Time: 25 Minutes
**Ingredients:**
- 25 Brussels sprouts, halved
- 2 mini sweet peppers, diced
- 1 yellow onion, diced
- 3 deli ham slices, diced
- 2 tbsp orange juice
- ¼ tsp salt
- 1 tsp orange zest

**Directions:**

1. Preheat air fryer to 350ºF. Mix the sprouts, sweet peppers, onion, deli ham, orange juice, and salt in a bowl. Transfer to the frying basket and Air Fry for 12 minutes, tossing once. Scatter with orange zest and serve.

# Zucchini Hash Browns

Servings: 4
Cooking Time: 20 Minutes
**Ingredients:**
- 2 shredded zucchinis
- 2 tbsp nutritional yeast
- 1 tsp allspice
- 1 egg white

**Directions:**

1. Preheat air fryer to 400°F. Combine zucchinis, nutritional yeast, allspice, and egg white in a bowl. Make 4 patties out of the mixture. Cut 4 pieces of parchment paper, put a patty on each foil, and fold in all sides to create a rectangle. Using a spatula, flatten them and spread them.
2. Then unwrap each foil and remove the hash browns onto the fryer and Air Fry for 12 minutes until golden brown and crispy, turning once. Serve right away.

# Bacon Puff Pastry Pinwheels

Servings: 8
Cooking Time: 10 Minutes
**Ingredients:**
- 1 sheet of puff pastry
- 2 tablespoons maple syrup
- ¼ cup brown sugar
- 8 slices bacon (not thick cut)
- coarsely cracked black pepper
- vegetable oil

**Directions:**

1. On a lightly floured surface, roll the puff pastry out into a square that measures roughly 10 inches wide by however long your bacon strips are (usually about 11 inches). Cut the pastry into eight even strips.
2. Brush the strips of pastry with the maple syrup and sprinkle the brown sugar on top, leaving 1 inch of dough exposed at the far end of each strip. Place a slice of bacon on each strip of puff pastry, letting 1/8-inch of the length of bacon hang over the edge of the pastry. Season generously with coarsely ground black pepper.
3. With the exposed end of the pastry strips away from you, roll the bacon and pastry strips up into pinwheels. Dab a little water on the exposed end of the pastry and pinch it to the pinwheel to seal the pastry shut.
4. Preheat the air fryer to 360°F.
5. Brush or spray the air fryer basket with a little vegetable oil. Place the pinwheels into the basket and air-fry at 360°F for 8 minutes. Turn the pinwheels over and air-fry for another 2 minutes to brown the bottom. Serve warm.

# Pizza Dough

Servings: 3
Cooking Time: 10 Minutes
**Ingredients:**

* 4 cups bread flour, pizza ("00") flour or all-purpose flour
* 1 teaspoon active dry yeast
* 2 teaspoons sugar
* 2 teaspoons salt
* 1½ cups water
* 1 tablespoon olive oil

**Directions:**

1. Combine the flour, yeast, sugar and salt in the bowl of a stand mixer. Add the olive oil to the flour mixture and start to mix using the dough hook attachment. As you're mixing, add 1¼ cups of the water, mixing until the dough comes together. Continue to knead the dough with the dough hook for another 10 minutes, adding enough water to the dough to get it to the right consistency.

2. Transfer the dough to a floured counter and divide it into 3 equal portions. Roll each portion into a ball. Lightly coat each dough ball with oil and transfer to the refrigerator, covered with plastic wrap. You can place them all on a baking sheet, or place each dough ball into its own oiled zipper sealable plastic bag or container. (You can freeze the dough balls at this stage, removing as much air as possible from the oiled bag.) Keep in the refrigerator for at least one day, or as long as five days.

3. When you're ready to use the dough, remove your dough from the refrigerator at least 1 hour prior to baking and let it sit on the counter, covered gently with plastic wrap.

# Blueberry Pannenkoek (dutch Pancake)

Servings: 4
Cooking Time: 30 Minutes
**Ingredients:**

* 3 eggs, beaten
* ½ cup buckwheat flour
* ½ cup milk
* ½ tsp vanilla
* 1 ½ cups blueberries, crushed
* 2 tbsp powdered sugar

**Directions:**

1. Preheat air fryer to 330°F. Mix together eggs, buckwheat flour, milk, and vanilla in a bowl. Pour the batter into a greased baking pan and add it to the fryer. Bake until the pancake is puffed and golden, 12-16 minutes. Remove the pan and flip the pancake over onto a plate. Add blueberries and powdered sugar as a topping and serve.

# Blueberry French Toast Sticks

Servings: 4
Cooking Time: 20 Minutes
**Ingredients:**

* 3 bread slices, cut into strips
* 1 tbsp butter, melted
* 2 eggs
* 1 tbsp milk
* 1 tbsp sugar
* ½ tsp vanilla extract
* 1 cup fresh blueberries
* 1 tbsp lemon juice

**Directions:**

1. Preheat air fryer to 380°F. After laying the bread strips on a plate, sprinkle some melted butter over each piece. Whisk the eggs, milk, vanilla, and sugar, then dip the bread in the mix. Place on a wire rack to let the batter drip. Put the bread strips in the air fryer and Air Fry for 5-7 minutes. Use tongs to flip them once and cook until golden. With a fork, smash the blueberries and lemon juice together. Spoon the blueberries sauce over the French sticks. Serve immediately.

# Peppered Maple Bacon Knots

Servings: 6
Cooking Time: 8 Minutes
**Ingredients:**

* 1 pound maple smoked center-cut bacon
* ¼ cup maple syrup
* ¼ cup brown sugar
* coarsely cracked black peppercorns

**Directions:**

1. Tie each bacon strip in a loose knot and place them on a baking sheet.

2. Combine the maple syrup and brown sugar in a bowl. Brush each knot generously with this mixture and sprinkle with coarsely cracked black pepper.

3. Preheat the air fryer to 390°F.

4. Air-fry the bacon knots in batches. Place one layer of knots in the air fryer basket and air-fry for 5 minutes. Turn the bacon knots over and air-fry for an additional 3 minutes.

5. Serve warm.

# Cinnamon Pumpkin Donuts

Servings: 6
Cooking Time: 30 Minutes
**Ingredients:**

- 1/3 cup canned pumpkin purée
- 1 cup flour
- 3 tbsp brown sugar
- ½ tsp ground cinnamon
- 1/8 tsp ground nutmeg
- 1 tsp baking powder
- 3 tbsp milk
- 2 tbsp butter, melted
- 1 large egg
- 3 tbsp powdered sugar

**Directions:**

1. Combine the flour, brown sugar, cinnamon, nutmeg, and baking powder in a bowl. Whisk the pumpkin, milk, butter, and egg white in another bowl. Pour the pumpkin mixture over the dry ingredients and stir. Add more milk or flour if necessary to make a soft dough.Cover your hands in flour, make 12 pieces from the dough, and form them into balls. Measure the frying basket, then cut foil or parchment paper about an inch smaller than the measurement. Poke holes in it and put it in the basket.

2. Preheat air fryer to 360°F. Set the donut holes in the basket and Air Fry for 5-7 minutes. Allow the donuts to chill for 5 minutes, then roll in powdered sugar. Serve.

# Mini Bacon Egg Quiches

Servings:6

Cooking Time: 30 Minutes
**Ingredients:**

- 3 eggs
- 2 tbsp heavy cream
- ¼ tsp Dijon mustard
- Salt and pepper to taste
- 3 oz cooked bacon, crumbled
- ¼ cup grated cheddar

**Directions:**

1. Preheat air fryer to 350°F. Beat the eggs with salt and pepper in a bowl until fluffy. Stir in heavy cream, mustard, cooked bacon, and cheese. Divide the mixture between 6 greased muffin cups and place them in the frying basket. Bake for 8-10 minutes. Let cool slightly before serving.

# Southwest Cornbread

Servings: 6
Cooking Time: 18 Minutes
**Ingredients:**

- cooking spray
- ½ cup yellow cornmeal
- ½ cup flour
- 2 teaspoons baking powder
- ½ teaspoon salt
- ½ cup frozen corn kernels, thawed and drained
- ¼ cup finely chopped onion
- 1 or 2 small jalapeño peppers, seeded and chopped
- 1 egg
- ½ cup milk
- 2 tablespoons melted butter
- 2 ounces sharp Cheddar cheese, grated

**Directions:**

1. Preheat air fryer to 360°F.

2. Spray air fryer baking pan with nonstick cooking spray.

3. In a medium bowl, stir together the cornmeal, flour, baking powder, and salt.

4. Stir in the corn, onion, and peppers.

5. In a small bowl, beat together the egg, milk, and butter. Stir into dry ingredients until well combined.

6. Spoon half the batter into prepared baking pan, spreading to edges. Top with grated cheese. Spoon

remaining batter on top of cheese and gently spread to edges of pan so it completely covers the cheese.

7. Cook at 360°F for 18 minutes, until cornbread is done and top is crispy brown.

## Holiday Breakfast Casserole

Servings:2
Cooking Time: 25 Minutes
**Ingredients:**
- ¼ cup cooked spicy breakfast sausage
- 5 eggs
- 2 tbsp heavy cream
- ½ tsp ground cumin
- Salt and pepper to taste
- ½ cup feta cheese crumbles
- 1 tomato, diced
- 1 can green chiles, including juice
- 1 zucchini, diced

**Directions:**
1. Preheat air fryer to 325°F. Mix all ingredients in a bowl and pour into a greased baking pan. Place the pan in the frying basket and Bake for 14 minutes. Let cool for 5 minutes before slicing. Serve right away.

## Sweet Potato & Mushroom Hash

Servings: 6
Cooking Time: 35 Minutes
**Ingredients:**
- 2 peeled sweet potatoes, cubed
- 4 oz baby Bella mushrooms, diced
- ½ red bell pepper, diced
- ½ red onion, diced
- 2 tbsp olive oil
- 1 garlic clove, minced
- Salt and pepper to taste
- ½ tbsp chopped marjoram

**Directions:**
1. Preheat air fryer to 380°F. Place all ingredients in a large bowl and toss until the vegetables are well coated.

Pour the vegetables into the frying basket. Bake for 8-10 minutes, then shake the vegetables. Cook for 8-10 more minutes. Serve and enjoy!

## Banana-strawberry Cakecups

Servings: 6
Cooking Time: 25 Minutes
**Ingredients:**
- ½ cup mashed bananas
- ¼ cup maple syrup
- ½ cup Greek yogurt
- 1 tsp vanilla extract
- 1 egg
- 1 ½ cups flour
- 1 tbsp cornstarch
- ½ tsp baking soda
- ½ tsp baking powder
- ½ tsp salt
- ½ cup strawberries, sliced

**Directions:**
1. Preheat air fryer to 360°F. Place the mashed bananas, maple syrup, yogurt, vanilla, and egg in a large bowl and mix until smooth. Sift in 1 ½ cups of the flour, baking soda, baking powder, and salt, then stir to combine.
2. In a small bowl, toss the strawberries with the cornstarch. Fold the mixture into the muffin batter. Divide the mixture evenly between greased muffin cups and place into the air frying basket. Bake for 12-15 minutes until golden brown on top and a toothpick inserted into the middle of one of the muffins comes out clean. Leave to cool for 5 minutes. Serve and enjoy!

## Cinnamon Sugar Donut Holes

Servings: 12
Cooking Time: 6 Minutes
**Ingredients:**
- 1 cup all-purpose flour
- 6 tablespoons cane sugar, divided
- 1 teaspoon baking powder
- 3 teaspoons ground cinnamon, divided
- ¼ teaspoon salt

- 1 large egg
- 1 teaspoon vanilla extract
- 2 tablespoons melted butter

**Directions:**
1. Preheat the air fryer to 370°F.
2. In a small bowl, combine the flour, 2 tablespoons of the sugar, the baking powder, 1 teaspoon of the cinnamon, and the salt. Mix well.
3. In a larger bowl, whisk together the egg, vanilla extract, and butter.
4. Slowly add the dry ingredients into the wet until all the ingredients are uniformly combined. Set the bowl inside the refrigerator for at least 30 minutes.
5. Before you're ready to cook, in a small bowl, mix together the remaining 4 tablespoons of sugar and 2 teaspoons of cinnamon.
6. Liberally spray the air fryer basket with olive oil mist so the donut holes don't stick to the bottom. Note: You do not want to use parchment paper in this recipe; it may burn if your air fryer is hotter than others.
7. Remove the dough from the refrigerator and divide it into 12 equal donut holes. You can use a 1-ounce serving scoop if you have one.
8. Roll each donut hole in the sugar and cinnamon mixture; then place in the air fryer basket. Repeat until all the donut holes are covered in the sugar and cinnamon mixture.
9. When the basket is full, cook for 6 minutes. Remove the donut holes from the basket using oven-safe tongs and let cool 5 minutes. Repeat until all 12 are cooked.

# Chocolate Almond Crescent Rolls

Servings: 4
Cooking Time: 8 Minutes
**Ingredients:**
- 1 (8-ounce) tube of crescent roll dough
- ⅔ cup semi-sweet or bittersweet chocolate chunks
- 1 egg white, lightly beaten
- ¼ cup sliced almonds
- powdered sugar, for dusting
- butter or oil

**Directions:**
1. Preheat the air fryer to 350°F.

2. Unwrap the crescent roll dough and separate it into triangles with the points facing away from you. Place a row of chocolate chunks along the bottom edge of the dough. (If you are using chips, make it a double row.) Roll the dough up around the chocolate and then place another row of chunks on the dough. Roll again and finish with one or two chocolate chunks. Be sure to leave the end free of chocolate so that it can adhere to the rest of the roll.
3. Brush the tops of the crescent rolls with the lightly beaten egg white and sprinkle the almonds on top, pressing them into the crescent dough so they adhere.
4. Brush the bottom of the air fryer basket with butter or oil and transfer the crescent rolls to the basket. Air-fry at 350°F for 8 minutes. Remove and let the crescent rolls cool before dusting with powdered sugar and serving.

# Seafood Quinoa Frittata

Servings: 4
Cooking Time: 30 Minutes
**Ingredients:**
- ½ cup cooked shrimp, chopped
- ½ cup cooked quinoa
- ½ cup baby spinach
- 4 eggs
- ½ tsp dried basil
- 1 anchovy, chopped
- ½ cup grated cheddar

**Directions:**
1. Preheat air fryer to 320°F. Add quinoa, shrimp, and spinach to a greased baking pan. Set aside. Beat eggs, anchovy, and basil in a bowl until frothy. Pour over the quinoa mixture, then top with cheddar cheese. Bake until the frittata is puffed and golden, 14-18 minutes. Serve.

# Banana Bread

Servings: 6
Cooking Time: 20 Minutes
**Ingredients:**
- cooking spray
- 1 cup white wheat flour
- ½ teaspoon baking powder
- ¼ teaspoon salt
- ¼ teaspoon baking soda
- 1 egg
- ½ cup mashed ripe banana
- ¼ cup plain yogurt
- ¼ cup pure maple syrup
- 2 tablespoons coconut oil
- ½ teaspoon pure vanilla extract

**Directions:**
1. Preheat air fryer to 330°F.
2. Lightly spray 6 x 6-inch baking dish with cooking spray.
3. In a medium bowl, mix together the flour, baking powder, salt, and soda.
4. In a separate bowl, beat the egg and add the mashed banana, yogurt, syrup, oil, and vanilla. Mix until well combined.
5. Pour liquid mixture into dry ingredients and stir gently to blend. Do not beat. Batter may be slightly lumpy.
6. Pour batter into baking dish and cook at 330°F for 20 minutes or until toothpick inserted in center of loaf comes out clean.

# Almond-pumpkin Porridge

Servings: 4
Cooking Time: 10 Minutes
**Ingredients:**
- 1 cup pumpkin seeds
- 2/3 cup chopped pecans
- 1/3 cup quick-cooking oats
- ¼ cup pumpkin purée
- ¼ cup diced pitted dates
- 1 tsp chia seeds
- 1 tsp sesame seeds
- 1 tsp dried berries
- 2 tbsp butter
- 2 tsp pumpkin pie spice
- ¼ cup honey
- 1 tbsp dark brown sugar
- ¼ cup almond flour
- Salt to taste

**Directions:**
1. Preheat air fryer at 350ºF. Combine the pumpkin seeds, pecans, oats, pumpkin purée, dates, chia seeds, sesame seeds, dried berries, butter, pumpkin pie spice, honey, sugar, almond flour, and salt in a bowl. Press mixture into a greased cake pan. Place cake pan in the frying basket and Bake for 5 minutes, stirring once. Let cool completely for 10 minutes before crumbling.

# Southern Sweet Cornbread

Servings: 6
Cooking Time: 17 Minutes
**Ingredients:**
- cooking spray
- ½ cup white cornmeal
- ½ cup flour
- 2 teaspoons baking powder
- ½ teaspoon salt
- 4 teaspoons sugar
- 1 egg
- 2 tablespoons oil
- ½ cup milk

**Directions:**
1. Preheat air fryer to 360°F.
2. Spray air fryer baking pan with nonstick cooking spray.
3. In a medium bowl, stir together the cornmeal, flour, baking powder, salt, and sugar.
4. In a small bowl, beat together the egg, oil, and milk. Stir into dry ingredients until well combined.
5. Pour batter into prepared baking pan.
6. Cook at 360°F for 17 minutes or until toothpick inserted in center comes out clean or with crumbs clinging.

# Beef , pork & Lamb Recipes

## French-style Pork Medallions

Servings: 4
Cooking Time: 25 Minutes
**Ingredients:**
- 1 lb pork medallions
- Salt and pepper to taste
- ½ tsp dried marjoram
- 2 tbsp butter
- 1 tbsp olive oil
- 1 tsp garlic powder
- 1 shallot, diced
- 1cup chicken stock
- 2 tbsp Dijon mustard
- 2 tbsp grainy mustard
- 1/3 cup heavy cream

**Directions:**
1. Preheat the air fryer to 350°F. Pound the pork medallions with a rolling pin to about ¼ inch thickness. Rub them with salt, pepper, garlic, and marjoram. Place into the greased frying basket and Bake for 7 minutes or until almost done. Remove and wipe the basket clean. Combine the butter, olive oil, shallot, and stock in a baking pan, and set it in the frying basket. Bake for 5 minutes or until the shallot is crispy and tender. Add the mustard and heavy cream and cook for 4 more minutes or until the mix starts to thicken. Then add the pork to the sauce and cook for 5 more minutes, or until the sauce simmers. Remove and serve warm.

## Lamb Chops In Currant Sauce

Servings: 4
Cooking Time: 30 Minutes
**Ingredients:**
- ½ cup chicken broth
- 2 tbsp red currant jelly
- 2 tbsp Dijon mustard
- 1 tbsp lemon juice
- ½ tsp dried thyme
- ½ tsp dried mint
- 8 lamb chops
- Salt and pepper to taste

**Directions:**
1. Preheat the air fryer to 375°F. Combine the broth, jelly, mustard, lemon juice, mint, and thyme and mix with a whisk until smooth. Sprinkle the chops with salt and pepper and brush with some of the broth mixture.
2. Set 4 chops in the frying basket in a single layer, then add a raised rack and lay the rest of the chops on top. Bake for 15-20 minutes. Then, lay them in a cake pan and add the chicken broth mix. Put in the fryer and Bake for 3-5 more minutes or until the sauce is bubbling and the chops are tender.

## Rosemary Lamb Chops

Servings: 4
Cooking Time: 6 Minutes
**Ingredients:**
- 8 lamb chops
- 1 tablespoon extra-virgin olive oil
- 1 teaspoon dried rosemary, crushed
- 2 cloves garlic, minced
- 1 teaspoon sea salt
- ¼ teaspoon black pepper

**Directions:**
1. In a large bowl, mix together the lamb chops, olive oil, rosemary, garlic, salt, and pepper. Let sit at room temperature for 10 minutes.
2. Meanwhile, preheat the air fryer to 380°F.
3. Cook the lamb chops for 3 minutes, flip them over, and cook for another 3 minutes.

# Carne Asada

Servings: 4
Cooking Time: 15 Minutes
**Ingredients:**
- 4 cloves garlic, minced
- 3 chipotle peppers in adobo, chopped
- ⅓ cup chopped fresh parsley
- ⅓ cup chopped fresh oregano
- 1 teaspoon ground cumin seed
- juice of 2 limes
- ⅓ cup olive oil
- 1 to 1½ pounds flank steak (depending on your appetites)
- salt
- tortillas and guacamole (optional – for serving)

**Directions:**
1. Make the marinade: Combine the garlic, chipotle, parsley, oregano, cumin, lime juice and olive oil in a non-reactive bowl. Coat the flank steak with the marinade and let it marinate for 30 minutes to 8 hours. (Don't leave the steak out of refrigeration for longer than 2 hours, however.)
2. Preheat the air fryer to 390°F.
3. Remove the steak from the marinade and place it in the air fryer basket. Season the steak with salt and air-fry for 15 minutes, turning the steak over halfway through the cooking time and seasoning again with salt. This should cook the steak to medium. Add or subtract two minutes for medium-well or medium-rare.
4. Remember to let the steak rest before slicing the meat against the grain. Serve with warm tortillas, guacamole and a fresh salsa like the Tomato-Corn Salsa below.

# Pork & Beef Egg Rolls

Servings: 8
Cooking Time: 8 Minutes
**Ingredients:**
- ¼ pound very lean ground beef
- ¼ pound lean ground pork
- 1 tablespoon soy sauce
- 1 teaspoon olive oil
- ½ cup grated carrots
- 2 green onions, chopped
- 2 cups grated Napa cabbage
- ¼ cup chopped water chestnuts
- ¼ teaspoon salt
- ¼ teaspoon garlic powder
- ¼ teaspoon black pepper
- 1 egg
- 1 tablespoon water
- 8 egg roll wraps
- oil for misting or cooking spray

**Directions:**
1. In a large skillet, brown beef and pork with soy sauce. Remove cooked meat from skillet, drain, and set aside.
2. Pour off any excess grease from skillet. Add olive oil, carrots, and onions. Sauté until barely tender, about 1 minute.
3. Stir in cabbage, cover, and cook for 1 minute or just until cabbage slightly wilts. Remove from heat.
4. In a large bowl, combine the cooked meats and vegetables, water chestnuts, salt, garlic powder, and pepper. Stir well. If needed, add more salt to taste.
5. Beat together egg and water in a small bowl.
6. Fill egg roll wrappers, using about ¼ cup of filling for each wrap. Roll up and brush all over with egg wash to seal. Spray very lightly with olive oil or cooking spray.
7. Place 4 egg rolls in air fryer basket and cook at 390°F for 4minutes. Turn over and cook 4 more minutes, until golden brown and crispy.
8. Repeat to cook remaining egg rolls.

# Garlic-buttered Rib Eye Steak

Servings: 2
Cooking Time: 25 Minutes
**Ingredients:**
- 1 lb rib eye steak
- Salt and pepper to taste
- 1 tbsp butter
- 1 tsp paprika
- 1 tbsp chopped rosemary
- 2 garlic cloves, minced
- 2 tbsp chopped parsley
- 1 tbsp chopped mint

**Directions:**
1. Preheat air fryer to 400°F. Sprinkle salt and pepper on both sides of the rib eye. Transfer the rib eye to the greased frying basket, then top with butter, mint, paprika, rosemary,

and garlic. Bake for 6 minutes, then flip the steak. Bake for another 6 minutes. For medium-rare, the steak needs to reach an internal temperature of 140°F. Allow resting for 5 minutes before slicing. Serve sprinkled with parsley and enjoy!

# Kentucky-style Pork Tenderloin

Servings:2
Cooking Time: 30 Minutes
**Ingredients:**
- 1 lb pork tenderloin, halved crosswise
- 1 tbsp smoked paprika
- 2 tsp ground cumin
- 1 tsp garlic powder
- 1 tsp shallot powder
- ¼ tsp chili pepper
- Salt and pepper to taste
- 1 tsp Italian seasoning
- 2 tbsp butter, melted
- 1 tsp Worcestershire sauce

**Directions:**
1. Preheat air fryer to 350ºF. In a shallow bowl, combine all spices. Set aside. In another bowl, whisk butter and Worcestershire sauce and brush over pork tenderloin. Sprinkle with the seasoning mix. Place pork in the lightly greased frying basket and Air Fry for 16 minutes, flipping once. Let sit onto a cutting board for 5 minutes before slicing. Serve immediately.

# Beef And Spinach Braciole

Servings: 4
Cooking Time: 92 Minutes
**Ingredients:**
- 7-inch oven-safe baking pan or casserole
- ½ onion, finely chopped
- 1 teaspoon olive oil
- ⅓ cup red wine
- 2 cups crushed tomatoes
- 1 teaspoon Italian seasoning
- ½ teaspoon garlic powder
- ¼ teaspoon crushed red pepper flakes
- 2 tablespoons chopped fresh parsley
- 2 top round steaks (about 1½ pounds)
- salt and freshly ground black pepper
- 2 cups fresh spinach, chopped
- 1 clove minced garlic
- ½ cup roasted red peppers, julienned
- ½ cup grated pecorino cheese
- ¼ cup pine nuts, toasted and rough chopped
- 2 tablespoons olive oil

**Directions:**
1. Preheat the air fryer to 400°F.
2. Toss the onions and olive oil together in a 7-inch metal baking pan or casserole dish. Air-fry at 400°F for 5 minutes, stirring a couple times during the cooking process. Add the red wine, crushed tomatoes, Italian seasoning, garlic powder, red pepper flakes and parsley and stir. Cover the pan tightly with aluminum foil, lower the air fryer temperature to 350°F and continue to air-fry for 15 minutes.
3. While the sauce is simmering, prepare the beef. Using a meat mallet, pound the beef until it is ¼-inch thick. Season both sides of the beef with salt and pepper. Combine the spinach, garlic, red peppers, pecorino cheese, pine nuts and olive oil in a medium bowl. Season with salt and freshly ground black pepper. Spread the mixture evenly over the steaks. Starting at one of the short ends, roll the beef around the filling, tucking in the sides as you roll to ensure the filling is completely enclosed. Secure the beef rolls with toothpicks.
4. Remove the baking pan with the sauce from the air fryer and set it aside. Preheat the air fryer to 400°F.
5. Brush or spray the beef rolls with a little olive oil and air-fry at 400°F for 12 minutes, rotating the beef during the cooking process for even browning. When the beef is browned, submerge the rolls into the sauce in the baking pan, cover the pan with foil and return it to the air fryer. Air-fry at 250°F for 60 minutes.
6. Remove the beef rolls from the sauce. Cut each roll into slices and serve with pasta, ladling some of the sauce overtop.

# Pork Taco Gorditas

Servings: 4
Cooking Time: 21 Minutes
**Ingredients:**

- 1 pound lean ground pork
- 2 tablespoons chili powder
- 2 tablespoons ground cumin
- 1 teaspoon dried oregano
- 2 teaspoons paprika
- 1 teaspoon garlic powder
- ½ cup water
- 1 (15-ounce) can pinto beans, drained and rinsed
- ½ cup taco sauce
- salt and freshly ground black pepper
- 2 cups grated Cheddar cheese
- 5 (12-inch) flour tortillas
- 4 (8-inch) crispy corn tortilla shells
- 4 cups shredded lettuce
- 1 tomato, diced
- ⅓ cup sliced black olives
- sour cream, for serving
- tomato salsa, for serving

**Directions:**

1. Preheat the air fryer to 400°F.
2. Place the ground pork in the air fryer basket and air-fry at 400°F for 10 minutes, stirring a few times during the cooking process to gently break up the meat. Combine the chili powder, cumin, oregano, paprika, garlic powder and water in a small bowl. Stir the spice mixture into the browned pork. Stir in the beans and taco sauce and air-fry for an additional minute. Transfer the pork mixture to a bowl. Season to taste with salt and freshly ground black pepper.
3. Sprinkle ½ cup of the shredded cheese in the center of four of the flour tortillas, making sure to leave a 2-inch border around the edge free of cheese and filling. Divide the pork mixture among the four tortillas, placing it on top of the cheese. Place a crunchy corn tortilla on top of the pork and top with shredded lettuce, diced tomatoes, and black olives. Cut the remaining flour tortilla into 4 quarters. These quarters of tortilla will serve as the bottom of the gordita. Place one quarter tortilla on top of each gordita and fold the edges of the bottom flour tortilla up over the sides, enclosing the filling. While holding the seams down, brush the bottom of the gordita with olive oil and place the seam side down on the countertop while you finish the remaining three gorditas.
4. Preheat the air fryer to 380°F.
5. Air-fry one gordita at a time. Transfer the gordita carefully to the air fryer basket, seam side down. Brush or spray the top tortilla with oil and air-fry for 5 minutes. Carefully turn the gordita over and air-fry for an additional 5 minutes, until both sides are browned. When finished air frying all four gorditas, layer them back into the air fryer for an additional minute to make sure they are all warm before serving with sour cream and salsa.

# Sriracha Pork Strips With Rice

Servings: 4
Cooking Time: 30 Minutes + Chilling Time
**Ingredients:**

- ½ cup lemon juice
- 2 tbsp lemon marmalade
- 1 tbsp avocado oil
- 1 tbsp tamari
- 2 tsp sriracha
- 1 tsp yellow mustard
- 1 lb pork shoulder strips
- 4 cups cooked white rice
- ¼ cup chopped cilantro
- 1 tsp black pepper

**Directions:**

1. Whisk the lemon juice, lemon marmalade, avocado oil, tamari, sriracha, and mustard in a bowl. Reserve half of the marinade. Toss pork strips with half of the marinade and let marinate covered in the fridge for 30 minutes.
2. Preheat air fryer at 350ºF. Place pork strips in the frying basket and Air Fry for 17 minutes, tossing twice. Transfer them to a bowl and stir in the remaining marinade. Serve over cooked rice and scatter with cilantro and pepper.

# Hungarian Pork Burgers

Servings: 4
Cooking Time: 30 Minutes

**Ingredients:**

- 8 sandwich buns, halved
- ½ cup mayonnaise
- 2 tbsp mustard
- 1 tbsp lemon juice
- ¼ cup sliced red cabbage
- ¼ cup grated carrots
- 1 lb ground pork
- ½ tsp Hungarian paprika
- 1 cup lettuce, torn
- 2 tomatoes, sliced

**Directions:**

1. Mix the mayonnaise, 1 tbsp of mustard, lemon juice, cabbage, and carrots in a bowl. Refrigerate for 10 minutes.
2. Preheat air fryer to 400°F. Toss the pork, remaining mustard, and paprika in a bowl, mix, then make 8 patties. Place them in the air fryer and Air Fry for 7-9 minutes, flipping once until cooked through. Put some lettuce on one bottom bun, then top with a tomato slice, one burger, and some cabbage mix. Put another bun on top and serve. Repeat for all burgers. Serve and enjoy!

# Blossom Bbq Pork Chops

Servings: 2
Cooking Time: 20 Minutes

**Ingredients:**

- 2 tbsp cherry preserves
- 1 tbsp honey
- 1 tbsp Dijon mustard
- 2 tsp light brown sugar
- 1 tsp Worcestershire sauce
- 1 tbsp lime juice
- 1 tbsp olive oil
- 2 cloves garlic, minced
- 1 tbsp chopped parsley
- 2 pork chops

**Directions:**

1. Mix all ingredients in a bowl. Toss in pork chops. Let marinate covered in the fridge for 30 minutes.

2. Preheat air fryer at 350°F. Place pork chops in the greased frying basket and Air Fry for 12 minutes, turning once. Let rest onto a cutting board for 5 minutes. Serve.

# Kochukaru Pork Lettuce Cups

Servings: 4
Cooking Time: 25 Minutes

**Ingredients:**

- 1 tsp kochukaru (chili pepper flakes)
- 12 baby romaine lettuce leaves
- 1 lb pork tenderloin, sliced
- Salt and pepper to taste
- 3 scallions, chopped
- 3 garlic cloves, crushed
- ¼ cup soy sauce
- 2 tbsp gochujang
- ½ tbsp light brown sugar
- ½ tbsp honey
- 1 tbsp grated fresh ginger
- 2 tbsp rice vinegar
- 1 tsp toasted sesame oil
- 2 ¼ cups cooked brown rice
- ½ tbsp sesame seeds
- 2 spring onions, sliced

**Directions:**

1. Mix the scallions, garlic, soy sauce, kochukaru, honey, brown sugar, and ginger in a small bowl. Mix well. Place the pork in a large bowl. Season with salt and pepper. Pour the marinade over the pork, tossing the meat in the marinade until coated. Cover the bowl with plastic wrap and allow to marinate overnight. When ready to cook,
2. Preheat air fryer to 400°F. Remove the pork from the bowl and discard the marinade. Place the pork in the greased frying basket and Air Fry for 10 minutes, flipping once until browned and cooked through. Meanwhile, prepare the gochujang sauce. Mix the gochujang, rice vinegar, and sesame oil until smooth. To make the cup, add 3 tbsp of brown rice on the lettuce leaf. Place a slice of pork on top, drizzle a tsp of gochujang sauce and sprinkle with some sesame seeds and spring onions. Wrap the lettuce over the mixture similar to a burrito. Serve warm.

# Lemon Pork Escalopes

Servings: 4

Cooking Time: 45 Minutes

**Ingredients:**

- 4 pork loin chops
- 1 cup breadcrumbs
- 2 eggs, beaten
- Salt and pepper to taste
- ½ tbsp thyme, chopped
- ½ tsp smoked paprika
- ½ tsp ground cumin
- 1 lemon, zested

**Directions:**

1. Preheat air fryer to 350°F. Mix the breadcrumbs, thyme, smoked paprika, cumin, lemon zest, salt, and pepper in a bowl. Add the pork chops and toss to coat. Dip in the beaten eggs, then dip again into the dry ingredients. Place the coated chops in the greased frying basket and Air Fry for 16-18 minutes, turning once. Serve and enjoy!

# Seedy Rib Eye Steak Bites

Servings: 4

Cooking Time: 20 Minutes

**Ingredients:**

- 1 lb rib eye steak, cubed
- 2 garlic cloves, minced
- 2 tbsp olive oil
- 1 tbsp thyme, chopped
- 1 tsp ground fennel seeds
- Salt and pepper to taste
- 1 onion, thinly sliced

**Directions:**

1. Preheat air fryer to 380°F. Place the steak, garlic, olive oil, thyme, fennel seeds, salt, pepper, and onion in a bowl. Mix until all of the beef and onion are well coated. Put the seasoned steak mixture into the frying basket. Roast for 10 minutes, stirring once. Let sit for 5 minutes. Serve.

# Traditional Moo Shu Pork Lettuce Wraps

Servings: 4

Cooking Time: 40 Minutes

**Ingredients:**

- ½ cup sliced shiitake mushrooms
- 1 lb boneless pork loin, cubed
- 3 tbsp cornstarch
- 2 tbsp rice vinegar
- 3 tbsp hoisin sauce
- 1 tsp oyster sauce
- 3 tsp sesame oil
- 1 tsp sesame seeds
- ¼ tsp ground ginger
- 1 egg
- 2 tbsp flour
- 1 bag coleslaw mix
- 1 cup chopped baby spinach
- 3 green onions, sliced
- 8 iceberg lettuce leaves

**Directions:**

1. Preheat air fryer at 350°F. Make a slurry by whisking 1 tbsp of cornstarch and 1 tbsp of water in a bowl. Set aside. Warm a saucepan over heat, add in rice vinegar, hoisin sauce, oyster sauce, 1 tsp of sesame oil, and ginger, and cook for 3 minutes, stirring often. Add in cornstarch slurry and cook for 1 minute. Set aside and let the mixture thicken. Beat the egg, flour, and the remaining cornstarch in a bowl. Set aside.

2. Dredge pork cubes in the egg mixture. Shake off any excess. Place them in the greased frying basket and Air Fry for 8 minutes, shaking once. Warm the remaining sesame oil in a skillet over medium heat. Add in coleslaw mix, baby spinach, green onions, and mushrooms and cook for 5 minutes until the coleslaw wilts. Turn the heat off. Add in cooked pork, pour in oyster sauce mixture, and toss until coated. Divide mixture between lettuce leaves, sprinkle with sesame seed, roll them up, and serve.

# Easy-peasy Beef Sliders

Servings:4
Cooking Time: 25 Minutes
**Ingredients:**
- 1 lb ground beef
- ¼ tsp cumin
- ¼ tsp mustard power
- 1/3 cup grated yellow onion
- ½ tsp smoked paprika
- Salt and pepper to taste

**Directions:**

1. Preheat air fryer to 350ºF. Combine the ground beef, cumin, mustard, onion, paprika, salt, and black pepper in a bowl. Form mixture into 8 patties and make a slight indentation in the middle of each. Place beef patties in the greased frying basket and Air Fry for 8-10 minutes, flipping once. Serve right away and enjoy!

# Chipotle Pork Meatballs

Servings:4
Cooking Time: 35 Minutes
**Ingredients:**
- 1 lb ground pork
- 1 egg
- ¼ cup chipotle sauce
- ¼ cup grated celery
- ¼ cup chopped parsley
- ¼ cup chopped cilantro
- ¼ cup flour
- ¼ tsp salt

**Directions:**

1. Preheat air fryer to 350ºF. In a large bowl, combine the ground pork, egg, chipotle sauce, celery, parsley, cilantro, flour, and salt. Form mixture into 16 meatballs. Place the meatballs in the lightly greased frying basket and Air Fry for 8-10 minutes, flipping once. Serve immediately!

# Citrus Pork Lettuce Wraps

Servings:4

Cooking Time: 35 Minutes
**Ingredients:**
- Salt and white pepper to taste
- 1 tbsp cornstarch
- 1 tbsp red wine vinegar
- 2 tbsp orange marmalade
- 1 tsp pulp-free orange juice
- 2 tsp olive oil
- ¼ tsp chili pepper
- ¼ tsp ground ginger
- 1 lb pork loin, cubed
- 8 iceberg lettuce leaves

**Directions:**

1. Create a slurry by whisking cornstarch and 1 tbsp of water in a bowl. Set aside. Place a small saucepan over medium heat. Add the red wine vinegar, orange marmalade, orange juice, olive oil, chili pepper, and ginger and cook for 3 minutes, stirring continuously. Mix in the slurry and simmer for 1 more minute. Turn the heat off and let it thicken, about3 minutes.

2. Preheat air fryer to 350ºF. Sprinkle the pork with salt and white pepper. Place them in the greased frying basket and Air Fry for 8-10 minutes until cooked through and browned, turning once. Transfer pork cubes to a bowl with the sauce and toss to coat. Serve in lettuce leaves.

# Steak Fingers

Servings: 4
Cooking Time: 8 Minutes
**Ingredients:**
- 4 small beef cube steaks
- salt and pepper
- ½ cup flour
- oil for misting or cooking spray

**Directions:**

1. Cut cube steaks into 1-inch-wide strips.
2. Sprinkle lightly with salt and pepper to taste.
3. Roll in flour to coat all sides.
4. Spray air fryer basket with cooking spray or oil.
5. Place steak strips in air fryer basket in single layer, very close together but not touching. Spray top of steak strips with oil or cooking spray.

39

6. Cook at 390°F for 4minutes, turn strips over, and spray with oil or cooking spray.

7. Cook 4 more minutes and test with fork for doneness. Steak fingers should be crispy outside with no red juices inside. If needed, cook an additional 4 minutes or until well done. (Don't eat beef cube steak rare.)

8. Repeat steps 5 through 7 to cook remaining strips.

# Easy Tex-mex Chimichangas

Servings: 2
Cooking Time: 8 Minutes

**Ingredients:**

- ¼ pound Thinly sliced deli roast beef, chopped
- ½ cup (about 2 ounces) Shredded Cheddar cheese or shredded Tex-Mex cheese blend
- ¼ cup Jarred salsa verde or salsa rojo
- ½ teaspoon Ground cumin
- ½ teaspoon Dried oregano
- 2 Burrito-size (12-inch) flour tortilla(s), not corn tortillas (gluten-free, if a concern)
- ⅔ cup Canned refried beans
- Vegetable oil spray

**Directions:**

1. Preheat the air fryer to 375°F .

2. Stir the roast beef, cheese, salsa, cumin, and oregano in a bowl until well mixed.

3. Lay a tortilla on a clean, dry work surface. Spread ⅓ cup of the refried beans in the center lower third of the tortilla(s), leaving an inch on either side of the spread beans.

4. For one chimichanga, spread all of the roast beef mixture on top of the beans. For two, spread half of the roast beef mixture on each tortilla.

5. At either "end" of the filling mixture, fold the sides of the tortilla up and over the filling, partially covering it. Starting with the unfolded side of the tortilla just below the filling, roll the tortilla closed. Fold and roll the second filled tortilla, as necessary.

6. Coat the exterior of the tortilla(s) with vegetable oil spray. Set the chimichanga(s) seam side down in the basket, with at least ½ inch air space between them if you're working with two. Air-fry undisturbed for 8 minutes, or until the tortilla is lightly browned and crisp.

7. Use kitchen tongs to gently transfer the chimichanga(s) to a wire rack. Cool for at last 5 minutes or up to 20 minutes before serving.

# Brie And Cranberry Burgers

Servings: 3
Cooking Time: 9 Minutes

**Ingredients:**

- 1 pound ground beef (80% lean)
- 1 tablespoon chopped fresh thyme
- 1 tablespoon Worcestershire sauce
- ½ teaspoon salt
- freshly ground black pepper
- 1 (4-ounce) wheel of Brie cheese, sliced
- handful of arugula
- 3 or 4 brioche hamburger buns (or potato hamburger buns), toasted
- ¼ to ½ cup whole berry cranberry sauce

**Directions:**

1. Combine the beef, thyme, Worcestershire sauce, salt and pepper together in a large bowl and mix well. Divide the meat into 4 (¼-pound) portions or 3 larger portions and then form them into burger patties, being careful not to over-handle the meat.

2. Preheat the air fryer to 390°F and pour a little water into the bottom of the air fryer drawer. (This will help prevent the grease that drips into the bottom drawer from burning and smoking.)

3. Transfer the burgers to the air fryer basket. Air-fry the burgers at 390°F for 5 minutes. Flip the burgers over and air-fry for another 2 minutes. Top each burger with a couple slices of brie and air-fry for another minute or two, just to soften the cheese.

4. Build the burgers by placing a few leaves of arugula on the bottom bun, adding the burger and a spoonful of cranberry sauce on top. Top with the other half of the hamburger bun and enjoy.

# Peppered Steak Bites

Servings: 4
Cooking Time: 14 Minutes
**Ingredients:**

- 1 pound sirloin steak, cut into 1-inch cubes
- ½ teaspoon coarse sea salt
- 1 teaspoon coarse black pepper
- 2 teaspoons Worcestershire sauce
- ½ teaspoon garlic powder
- ¼ teaspoon red pepper flakes
- ¼ cup chopped parsley

**Directions:**

1. Preheat the air fryer to 390°F.
2. In a large bowl, place the steak cubes and toss with the salt, pepper, Worcestershire sauce, garlic powder, and red pepper flakes.
3. Pour the steak into the air fryer basket and cook for 10 to 14 minutes, depending on how well done you prefer your bites. Starting at the 8-minute mark, toss the steak bites every 2 minutes to check for doneness.
4. When the steak is cooked, remove it from the basket to a serving bowl and top with the chopped parsley. Allow the steak to rest for 5 minutes before serving.

# Barbecue-style Beef Cube Steak

Servings: 2
Cooking Time: 14 Minutes
**Ingredients:**

- 2 4-ounce beef cube steak(s)
- 2 cups (about 8 ounces) Fritos (original flavor) or a generic corn chip equivalent, crushed to crumbs (see here)
- 6 tablespoons Purchased smooth barbecue sauce, any flavor (gluten-free, if a concern)

**Directions:**

1. Preheat the air fryer to 375°F .
2. Spread the Fritos crumbs in a shallow soup plate or a small pie plate. Rub the barbecue sauce onto both sides of the steak(s). Dredge the steak(s) in the Fritos crumbs to coat well and thoroughly, turning several times and pressing down to get the little bits to adhere to the meat.
3. When the machine is at temperature, set the steak(s) in the basket. Leave as much air space between them as

possible if you're working with more than one piece of beef. Air-fry undisturbed for 12 minutes, or until lightly brown and crunchy. If the machine is at 360°F, you may need to add 2 minutes to the cooking time.
4. Use kitchen tongs to transfer the steak(s) to a wire rack. Cool for 5 minutes before serving.

# Balsamic Beef & Veggie Skewers

Servings: 4
Cooking Time: 25 Minutes
**Ingredients:**

- 2 tbsp balsamic vinegar
- 2 tsp olive oil
- ½ tsp dried oregano
- Salt and pepper to taste
- ¾ lb round steak, cubed
- 1 red bell pepper, sliced
- 1 yellow bell pepper, sliced
- 1 cup cherry tomatoes

**Directions:**

1. Preheat air fryer to 390°F. Put the balsamic vinegar, olive oil, oregano, salt, and black pepper in a bowl and stir. Toss the steak in and allow to marinate for 10 minutes. Poke 8 metal skewers through the beef, bell peppers, and cherry tomatoes, alternating ingredients as you go. Place the skewers in the air fryer and Air Fry for 5-7 minutes, turning once until the beef is golden and cooked through and the veggies are tender. Serve and enjoy!

# Boneless Ribeyes

Servings: 2
Cooking Time: 10-15 Minutes
**Ingredients:**

- 2 8-ounce boneless ribeye steaks
- 4 teaspoons Worcestershire sauce
- ½ teaspoon garlic powder
- pepper
- 4 teaspoons extra virgin olive oil
- salt

**Directions:**

1. Season steaks on both sides with Worcestershire sauce. Use the back of a spoon to spread evenly.
2. Sprinkle both sides of steaks with garlic powder and coarsely ground black pepper to taste.
3. Drizzle both sides of steaks with olive oil, again using the back of a spoon to spread evenly over surfaces.
4. Allow steaks to marinate for 30minutes.
5. Place both steaks in air fryer basket and cook at 390°F for 5minutes.
6. Turn steaks over and cook until done:
7. Medium rare: additional 5 minutes
8. Medium: additional 7 minutes
9. Well done: additional 10 minutes
10. Remove steaks from air fryer basket and let sit 5minutes. Salt to taste and serve.

## Steakhouse Filets Mignons

Servings: 3
Cooking Time: 12-15 Minutes
**Ingredients:**
- ¾ ounce Dried porcini mushrooms
- ¼ teaspoon Granulated white sugar
- ¼ teaspoon Ground white pepper
- ¼ teaspoon Table salt
- 6 ¼-pound filets mignons or beef tenderloin steaks
- 6 Thin-cut bacon strips (gluten-free, if a concern)

**Directions:**
1. Preheat the air fryer to 400°F.
2. Grind the dried mushrooms in a clean spice grinder until powdery. Add the sugar, white pepper, and salt. Grind to blend.
3. Rub this mushroom mixture into both cut sides of each filet. Wrap the circumference of each filet with a strip of bacon. (It will loop around the beef about 1½ times.)
4. Set the filets mignons in the basket on their sides with the bacon seam side down. Do not let the filets touch; keep at least ¼ inch open between them. Air-fry undisturbed for 12 minutes for rare, or until an instant-read meat thermometer inserted into the center of a filet registers 125°F (not USDA-approved); 13 minutes for medium-rare, or until an instant-read meat thermometer inserted into the center of a filet registers 132°F (not USDA-approved); or 15 minutes for medium, or until an instant-read meat thermometer inserted into the center of a filet registers 145°F (USDA-approved).

5. Use kitchen tongs to transfer the filets to a wire rack, setting them cut side down. Cool for 5 minutes before serving.

## Pork Loin

Servings: 8
Cooking Time: 50 Minutes
**Ingredients:**
- 1 tablespoon lime juice
- 1 tablespoon orange marmalade
- 1 teaspoon coarse brown mustard
- 1 teaspoon curry powder
- 1 teaspoon dried lemongrass
- 2-pound boneless pork loin roast
- salt and pepper
- cooking spray

**Directions:**
1. Mix together the lime juice, marmalade, mustard, curry powder, and lemongrass.
2. Rub mixture all over the surface of the pork loin. Season to taste with salt and pepper.
3. Spray air fryer basket with nonstick spray and place pork roast diagonally in basket.
4. Cook at 360°F for approximately 50 minutes, until roast registers 130°F on a meat thermometer.
5. Wrap roast in foil and let rest for 10minutes before slicing.

# Flank Steak With Roasted Peppers And Chimichurri

Servings: 4
Cooking Time: 22 Minutes
**Ingredients:**

- 2 cups flat-leaf parsley leaves
- ¼ cup fresh oregano leaves
- 3 cloves garlic
- ½ cup olive oil
- ¼ cup red wine vinegar
- ½ teaspoon salt
- freshly ground black pepper
- ¼ teaspoon crushed red pepper flakes
- ½ teaspoon ground cumin
- 1 pound flank steak
- 1 red bell pepper, cut into strips
- 1 yellow bell pepper, cut into strips

**Directions:**

1. Make the chimichurri sauce by chopping the parsley, oregano and garlic in a food processor. Add the olive oil, vinegar and seasonings and process again. Pour half of the sauce into a shallow dish with the flank steak and set the remaining sauce aside. Pierce the flank steak with a needle-style meat tenderizer or a paring knife and marinate the steak for 2 to 24 hours in the refrigerator. When you are ready to cook, remove the steak from the refrigerator and let it sit at room temperature for 30 minutes.
2. Preheat the air fryer to 400°F.
3. Cut the flank steak in half so that it fits more easily into the air fryer and transfer both pieces to the air fryer basket. Air-fry for 14 minutes, depending on how you like your steak cooked (10 minutes will give you medium for a 1-inch thick flank steak). Flip the steak over halfway through the cooking time.
4. When the flank steak is cooked to your liking, transfer it to a cutting board, loosely tent with foil and let it rest while you cook the peppers.
5. Toss the peppers in a little olive oil, salt and freshly ground black pepper and transfer them to the air fryer basket.

Air-fry at 400°F for 8 minutes, shaking the basket once or twice throughout the cooking process. To serve, slice the flank steak against the grain of the meat and top with the roasted peppers. Drizzle the reserved chimichurri sauce on top, thinning the sauce with another tablespoon of olive oil if desired.

# Stuffed Pork Chops

Servings: 4
Cooking Time: 12 Minutes
**Ingredients:**

- 4 boneless pork chops
- ½ teaspoon salt
- ½ teaspoon black pepper
- ¼ teaspoon paprika
- 1 cup frozen spinach, defrosted and squeezed dry
- 2 cloves garlic, minced
- 2 ounces cream cheese
- ¼ cup grated Parmesan cheese
- 1 tablespoon extra-virgin olive oil

**Directions:**

1. Pat the pork chops with a paper towel. Make a slit in the side of each pork chop to create a pouch.
2. Season the pork chops with the salt, pepper, and paprika.
3. In a small bowl, mix together the spinach, garlic, cream cheese, and Parmesan cheese.
4. Divide the mixture into fourths and stuff the pork chop pouches. Secure the pouches with toothpicks.
5. Preheat the air fryer to 400°F.
6. Place the stuffed pork chops in the air fryer basket and spray liberally with cooking spray. Cook for 6 minutes, flip and coat with more cooking spray, and cook another 6 minutes. Check to make sure the meat is cooked to an internal temperature of 145°F. Cook the pork chops in batches, as needed.

# Poultry Recipes

## Cheesy Chicken Tenders

Servings: 4
Cooking Time: 25 Minutes
**Ingredients:**

- 1 cup grated Parmesan cheese
- ¼ cup grated cheddar
- 1 ¼ lb chicken tenders
- 1 egg, beaten
- 2 tbsp milk
- Salt and pepper to taste
- ½ tsp garlic powder
- 1 tsp dried thyme
- ¼ tsp shallot powder

**Directions:**

1.  Preheat the air fryer to 400°F. Stir the egg and milk until combined. Mix the salt, pepper, garlic, thyme, shallot, cheddar cheese, and Parmesan cheese on a plate. Dip the chicken in the egg mix, then in the cheese mix, and press to coat. Lay the tenders in the frying basket in a single layer. Add a raised rack to cook more at one time. Spray all with oil and Bake for 12-16 minutes, flipping once halfway through cooking. Serve hot.

## Crunchy Chicken Strips

Servings: 4
Cooking Time: 40 Minutes
**Ingredients:**

- 1 chicken breast, sliced into strips
- 1 tbsp grated Parmesan cheese
- 1 cup breadcrumbs
- 1 tbsp chicken seasoning
- 2 eggs, beaten
- Salt and pepper to taste

**Directions:**

1.  Preheat air fryer to 350°F. Mix the breadcrumbs, Parmesan cheese, chicken seasoning, salt, and pepper in a mixing bowl. Coat the chicken with the crumb mixture, then dip in the beaten eggs. Finally, coat again with the dry ingredients. Arrange the coated chicken pieces on the greased frying basket and Air Fry for 15 minutes. Turn over halfway through cooking and cook for another 15 minutes. Serve immediately.

## Basic Chicken Breasts(2)

Servings:4
Cooking Time: 15 Minutes
**Ingredients:**

- 2 tsp olive oil
- 2 chicken breasts
- Salt and pepper to taste
- ½ tsp garlic powder
- ½ tsp rosemary

**Directions:**

1.  Preheat air fryer to 350°F. Rub the chicken breasts with olive oil over tops and bottom and sprinkle with garlic powder, rosemary, salt, and pepper. Place the chicken in the frying basket and Air Fry for 9 minutes, flipping once. Let rest onto a serving plate for 5 minutes before cutting into cubes. Serve and enjoy!

## Guajillo Chile Chicken Meatballs

Servings:4
Cooking Time: 30 Minutes
**Ingredients:**

- 1 lb ground chicken
- 1 large egg
- ½ cup bread crumbs
- 1 tbsp sour cream
- 2 tsp brown mustard
- 2 tbsp grated onion
- 2 tbsp tomato paste
- 1 tsp ground cumin
- 1 tsp guajillo chile powder
- 2 tbsp olive oil

**Directions:**

1. Preheat air fryer to 350ºF. Mix the ground chicken, egg, bread crumbs, sour cream, mustard, onion, tomato paste, cumin, and chili powder in a bowl. Form into 16 meatballs. Place the meatballs in the greased frying basket and Air Fry for 8-10 minutes, shaking once until browned and cooked through. Serve immediately.

## Cajun Chicken Livers

Servings: 2
Cooking Time: 45 Minutes
**Ingredients:**
- 1 lb chicken livers, rinsed, connective tissue discarded
- 1 cup whole milk
- ½ cup cornmeal
- 3/4 cup flour
- 1 tsp salt and black pepper
- 1 tsp Cajun seasoning
- 2 eggs
- 1 ½ cups bread crumbs
- 1 tbsp olive oil
- 2 tbsp chopped parsley

**Directions:**
1. Pat chicken livers dry with paper towels, then transfer them to a small bowl and pour in the milk and black pepper. Let sit covered in the fridge for 2 hours.
2. Preheat air fryer at 375ºF. In a bowl, combine cornmeal, flour, salt, and Cajun seasoning. In another bowl, beat the eggs, and in a third bowl, add bread crumbs. Dip chicken livers first in the cornmeal mixture, then in the egg, and finally in the bread crumbs. Place chicken livers in the greased frying basket, brush the tops lightly with olive oil, and Air Fry for 16 minutes, turning once. Serve right away sprinkled with parsley.

## Chicken Wings Al Ajillo

Servings:4
Cooking Time: 35 Minutes
**Ingredients:**
- 2 lb chicken wings, split at the joint
- 2 tbsp melted butter
- 2 tbsp grated Cotija cheese

- 4 cloves garlic, minced
- ½ tbsp hot paprika
- ¼ tsp salt

**Directions:**
1. Preheat air fryer to 250ºF. Coat the chicken wings with 1 tbsp of butter. Place them in the basket and Air Fry for 12 minutes, tossing once. In another bowl, whisk 1 tbsp of butter, Cotija cheese, garlic, hot paprika, and salt. Reserve. Increase temperature to 400ºF. Air Fry wings for 10 more minutes, tossing twice. Transfer them to the bowl with the sauce, and toss to coat. Serve immediately.

## Super-simple Herby Turkey

Servings: 4
Cooking Time: 35 Minutes
**Ingredients:**
- 2 turkey tenderloins
- 2 tbsp olive oil
- Salt and pepper to taste
- 2 tbsp minced rosemary
- 1 tbsp minced thyme
- 1 tbsp minced sage

**Directions:**
1. Preheat the air fryer to 350°F. Brush the tenderloins with olive oil and sprinkle with salt and pepper. Mix rosemary, thyme, and sage, then rub the seasoning onto the meat. Put the tenderloins in the frying basket and Bake for 22-27 minutes, flipping once until cooked through. Lay the turkey on a serving plate, cover with foil, and let stand for 5 minutes. Slice before serving.

## Maple Bacon Wrapped Chicken Breasts

Servings: 2
Cooking Time: 18 Minutes
**Ingredients:**
- 2 (6-ounce) boneless, skinless chicken breasts
- 2 tablespoons maple syrup, divided
- freshly ground black pepper

- 6 slices thick-sliced bacon
- fresh celery or parsley leaves
- Ranch Dressing:
- ¼ cup mayonnaise
- ¼ cup buttermilk
- ¼ cup Greek yogurt
- 1 tablespoon chopped fresh chives
- 1 tablespoon chopped fresh parsley
- 1 tablespoon chopped fresh dill
- 1 tablespoon lemon juice
- salt and freshly ground black pepper

**Directions:**

1. Brush the chicken breasts with half the maple syrup and season with freshly ground black pepper. Wrap three slices of bacon around each chicken breast, securing the ends with toothpicks.

2. Preheat the air fryer to 380°F.

3. Air-fry the chicken for 6 minutes. Then turn the chicken breasts over, pour more maple syrup on top and air-fry for another 6 minutes. Turn the chicken breasts one more time, brush the remaining maple syrup all over and continue to air-fry for a final 6 minutes.

4. While the chicken is cooking, prepare the dressing by combining all the dressing ingredients together in a bowl.

5. When the chicken has finished cooking, remove the toothpicks and serve each breast with a little dressing drizzled over each one. Scatter lots of fresh celery or parsley leaves on top.

# Chicken Parmigiana

Servings: 2
Cooking Time: 35 Minutes
**Ingredients:**

- 2 chicken breasts
- 1 cup breadcrumbs
- 2 eggs, beaten
- Salt and pepper to taste
- 1 tbsp dried basil
- 1 cup passata
- 2 provolone cheese slices
- 1 tbsp Parmesan cheese

**Directions:**

1. Preheat air fryer to 350°F. Mix the breadcrumbs, basil, salt, and pepper in a mixing bowl. Coat the chicken breasts with the crumb mixture, then dip in the beaten eggs. Finally, coat again with the dry ingredients. Arrange the coated chicken breasts on the greased frying basket and Air Fry for 20 minutes. At the 10-minutes mark, turn the breasts over and cook for the remaining 10 minutes.

2. Pour half of the passata into a baking pan. When the chicken is ready, remove it to the passata-covered pan. Pour the remaining passata over the fried chicken and arrange the provolone cheese slices on top and sprinkle with Parmesan cheese. Bake for 5 minutes until the chicken is crisped and the cheese melted and lightly toasted. Serve.

# Chicken Cordon Bleu Patties

Servings: 4
Cooking Time: 30 Minutes
**Ingredients:**

- 1/3 cup grated Fontina cheese
- 3 tbsp milk
- 1/3 cup bread crumbs
- 1 egg, beaten
- ½ tsp dried parsley
- Salt and pepper to taste
- 1 ¼ lb ground chicken
- ¼ cup finely chopped ham

**Directions:**

1. Preheat air fryer to 350°F. Mix milk, breadcrumbs, egg, parsley, salt and pepper in a bowl. Using your hands, add the chicken and gently mix until just combined. Divide into 8 portions and shape into thin patties. Place on waxed paper. On 4 of the patties, top with ham and Fontina cheese, then place another patty on top of that. Gently pinch the edges together so that none of the ham or cheese is peeking out. Arrange the burgers in the greased frying basket and Air Fry until cooked through, for 14-16 minutes. Serve and enjoy!

# Tortilla Crusted Chicken Breast

Servings: 2
Cooking Time: 12 Minutes
**Ingredients:**

- ⅓ cup flour
- 1 teaspoon salt
- 1½ teaspoons chili powder
- 1 teaspoon ground cumin
- freshly ground black pepper
- 1 egg, beaten
- ¾ cup coarsely crushed yellow corn tortilla chips
- 2 (3- to 4-ounce) boneless chicken breasts
- vegetable oil
- ½ cup salsa
- ½ cup crumbled queso fresco
- fresh cilantro leaves
- sour cream or guacamole (optional)

**Directions:**

1. Set up a dredging station with three shallow dishes. Combine the flour, salt, chili powder, cumin and black pepper in the first shallow dish. Beat the egg in the second shallow dish. Place the crushed tortilla chips in the third shallow dish.
2. Dredge the chicken in the spiced flour, covering all sides of the breast. Then dip the chicken into the egg, coating the chicken completely. Finally, place the chicken into the tortilla chips and press the chips onto the chicken to make sure they adhere to all sides of the breast. Spray the coated chicken breasts on both sides with vegetable oil.
3. Preheat the air fryer to 380°F.
4. Air-fry the chicken for 6 minutes. Then turn the chicken breasts over and air-fry for another 6 minutes. (Increase the cooking time if you are using chicken breasts larger than 3 to 4 ounces.)
5. When the chicken has finished cooking, serve each breast with a little salsa, the crumbled queso fresco and cilantro as the finishing touch. Serve some sour cream and/or guacamole at the table, if desired.

# Chicken Burgers With Blue Cheese Sauce

Servings: 4
Cooking Time: 40 Minutes

**Ingredients:**

- ¼ cup crumbled blue cheese
- ¼ cup sour cream
- 2 tbsp mayonnaise
- 1 tbsp red hot sauce
- Salt to taste
- 3 tbsp buffalo wing sauce
- 1 lb ground chicken
- 2 tbsp grated carrot
- 2 tbsp diced celery
- 1 egg white

**Directions:**

1. Whisk the blue cheese, sour cream, mayonnaise, red hot sauce, salt, and 1 tbsp of buffalo sauce in a bowl. Let sit covered in the fridge until ready to use.
2. Preheat air fryer at 350°F. In another bowl, combine the remaining ingredients. Form mixture into 4 patties, making a slight indentation in the middle of each. Place patties in the greased frying basket and Air Fry for 13 minutes until you reach your desired doneness, flipping once. Serve with the blue cheese sauce.

# Asian-style Orange Chicken

Servings: 4
Cooking Time: 25 Minutes
**Ingredients:**

- 1 lb chicken breasts, cubed
- Salt and pepper to taste
- 6 tbsp cornstarch
- 1 cup orange juice
- ¼ cup orange marmalade
- ¼ cup ketchup
- ½ tsp ground ginger
- 2 tbsp soy sauce
- 1 1/3 cups edamame beans

**Directions:**

1. Preheat the air fryer to 375°F. Sprinkle the cubes with salt and pepper. Coat with 4 tbsp of cornstarch and set aside on a wire rack. Mix the orange juice, marmalade, ketchup, ginger, soy sauce, and the remaining cornstarch in a cake pan, then stir in the beans. Set the pan in the frying basket and Bake for 5-8 minutes, stirring once during cooking until

the sauce is thick and bubbling. Remove from the fryer and set aside. Put the chicken in the frying basket and fry for 10-12 minutes, shaking the basket once. Stir the chicken into the sauce and beans in the pan. Return to the fryer and reheat for 2 minutes.

## **Chipotle Chicken Drumsticks**

Servings: 4
Cooking Time: 40 Minutes
**Ingredients:**
- 1 can chipotle chilies packed in adobe sauce
- 2 tbsp grated Mexican cheese
- 6 chicken drumsticks
- 1 egg, beaten
- ½ cup bread crumbs
- 1 tbsp corn flakes
- Salt and pepper to taste

**Directions:**
1. Preheat air fryer to 350°F. Place the chilies in the sauce in your blender and pulse until a fine paste is formed. Transfer to a bowl and add the beaten egg. Combine thoroughly. Mix the breadcrumbs, Mexican cheese, corn flakes, salt, and pepper in a separate bowl, and set aside.
2. Coat the chicken drumsticks with the crumb mixture, then dip into the bowl with wet ingredients, then dip again into the dry ingredients. Arrange the chicken drumsticks on the greased frying basket in a single flat layer. Air Fry for 14-16 minutes, turning each chicken drumstick over once. Serve warm.

## **Chicken Schnitzel Dogs**

Servings: 4
Cooking Time: 10 Minutes
**Ingredients:**
- ½ cup flour
- ½ teaspoon salt
- 1 teaspoon marjoram
- 1 teaspoon dried parsley flakes
- ½ teaspoon thyme
- 1 egg
- 1 teaspoon lemon juice

- 1 teaspoon water
- 1 cup breadcrumbs
- 4 chicken tenders, pounded thin
- oil for misting or cooking spray
- 4 whole-grain hotdog buns
- 4 slices Gouda cheese
- 1 small Granny Smith apple, thinly sliced
- ½ cup shredded Napa cabbage
- coleslaw dressing

**Directions:**
1. In a shallow dish, mix together the flour, salt, marjoram, parsley, and thyme.
2. In another shallow dish, beat together egg, lemon juice, and water.
3. Place breadcrumbs in a third shallow dish.
4. Cut each of the flattened chicken tenders in half lengthwise.
5. Dip flattened chicken strips in flour mixture, then egg wash. Let excess egg drip off and roll in breadcrumbs. Spray both sides with oil or cooking spray.
6. Cook at 390°F for 5minutes. Spray with oil, turn over, and spray other side.
7. Cook for 3 to 5minutes more, until well done and crispy brown.
8. To serve, place 2 schnitzel strips on bottom of each hot dog bun. Top with cheese, sliced apple, and cabbage. Drizzle with coleslaw dressing and top with other half of bun.

## **Indian Chicken Tandoori**

Servings: 2
Cooking Time: 35 Minutes
**Ingredients:**
- 2 chicken breasts, cubed
- ½ cup hung curd
- 1 tsp turmeric powder
- 1 tsp red chili powder
- 1 tsp chaat masala powder
- Pinch of salt

**Directions:**
1. Preheat air fryer to 350°F. Mix the hung curd, turmeric, red chili powder, chaat masala powder, and salt in a mixing

bowl. Stir until the mixture is free of lumps. Coat the chicken with the mixture, cover, and refrigerate for 30 minutes to marinate. Place the marinated chicken chunks in a baking pan and drizzle with the remaining marinade. Bake for 25 minutes until the chicken is juicy and spiced. Serve warm.

## Granny Pesto Chicken Caprese

Servings: 4
Cooking Time: 30 Minutes
**Ingredients:**
- 2 tbsp grated Parmesan cheese
- 4 oz fresh mozzarella cheese, thinly sliced
- 16 grape tomatoes, halved
- 4 garlic cloves, minced
- 1 tsp olive oil
- Salt and pepper to taste
- 4 chicken cutlets
- 1 tbsp prepared pesto
- 1 large egg, beaten
- ½ cup bread crumbs
- 2 tbsp Italian seasoning
- 1 tsp balsamic vinegar
- 2 tbsp chopped fresh basil

**Directions:**
1. Preheat air fryer to 400°F. In a bowl, coat the tomatoes with garlic, olive oil, salt and pepper. Air Fry for 5 minutes, shaking them twice. Set aside when soft.
2. Place the cutlets between two sheets of parchment paper. Pound the chicken to ¼-inch thickness using a meat mallet. Season on both sides with salt and pepper. Spread an even coat of pesto. Put the beaten egg in a shallow bowl. Mix the crumbs, Italian seasoning, and Parmesan in a second shallow bowl. Dip the chicken in the egg bowl, and then in the crumb mix. Press the crumbs so that they stick to the chicken.
3. Place the chicken in the greased frying basket. Air Fry the chicken for 6-8 minutes, flipping once until golden and cooked through. Put 1 oz of mozzarella and ¼ of the tomatoes on top of each cutlet. When all of the cutlets are cooked, return them to the frying basket and melt the cheese for 2 minutes. Remove from the fryer, drizzle with balsamic vinegar and basil on top.

## Teriyaki Chicken Legs

Servings: 2
Cooking Time: 20 Minutes
**Ingredients:**
- 4 tablespoons teriyaki sauce
- 1 tablespoon orange juice
- 1 teaspoon smoked paprika
- 4 chicken legs
- cooking spray

**Directions:**
1. Mix together the teriyaki sauce, orange juice, and smoked paprika. Brush on all sides of chicken legs.
2. Spray air fryer basket with nonstick cooking spray and place chicken in basket.
3. Cook at 360°F for 6minutes. Turn and baste with sauce. Cook for 6 moreminutes, turn and baste. Cook for 8 minutes more, until juices run clear when chicken is pierced with a fork.

## Pesto Chicken Cheeseburgers

Servings:4
Cooking Time: 40 Minutes
**Ingredients:**
- ¼ cup shredded Pepper Jack cheese
- 1 lb ground chicken
- 2 tbsp onion
- ¼ cup chopped parsley
- 1 egg white, beaten
- 1 tbsp pesto
- Salt and pepper to taste

**Directions:**
1. Preheat air fryer to 350ºF. Combine ground chicken, onion, cheese, parsley, egg white, salt, and pepper in a bowl. Make 4 patties out of the mixture. Place them in the greased frying basket and Air Fry for 12-14 minutes until golden, flipping once. Serve topped with pesto.

# Intense Buffalo Chicken Wings

Servings: 2
Cooking Time: 40 Minutes
**Ingredients:**
- 8 chicken wings
- ½ cup melted butter
- 2 tbsp Tabasco sauce
- ½ tbsp lemon juice
- 1 tbsp Worcestershire sauce
- 2 tsp cayenne pepper
- 1 tsp garlic powder
- 1 tsp lemon zest
- Salt and pepper to taste

**Directions:**
1. Preheat air fryer to 350°F. Place the melted butter, Tabasco, lemon juice, Worcestershire sauce, cayenne, garlic powder, lemon zest, salt, and pepper in a bowl and stir to combine. Dip the chicken wings into the mixture, coating thoroughly. Lay the coated chicken wings on the foil-lined frying basket in an even layer. Air Fry for 16-18 minutes. Shake the basket several times during cooking until the chicken wings are crispy brown. Serve.

# Popcorn Chicken Tenders With Vegetables

Servings: 4
Cooking Time: 30 Minutes
**Ingredients:**
- 2 tbsp cooked popcorn, ground
- Salt and pepper to taste
- 1 lb chicken tenders
- ½ cup bread crumbs
- ½ tsp dried thyme
- 1 tbsp olive oil
- 2 carrots, sliced
- 12 baby potatoes

**Directions:**
1. Preheat air fryer to 380°F. Season the chicken tenders with salt and pepper. In a shallow bowl, mix the crumbs, popcorn, thyme, and olive oil until combined. Coat the chicken with mixture. Press firmly, so the crumbs adhere. Arrange the carrots and baby potatoes in the greased frying basket and top them with the chicken tenders. Bake for 9-10 minutes. Shake the basket and continue cooking for another 9-10 minutes, until the vegetables are tender. Serve and enjoy!

# Buttermilk-fried Drumsticks

Servings: 2
Cooking Time: 25 Minutes
**Ingredients:**
- 1 egg
- ½ cup buttermilk
- ¾ cup self-rising flour
- ¾ cup seasoned panko breadcrumbs
- 1 teaspoon salt
- ¼ teaspoon ground black pepper (to mix into coating)
- 4 chicken drumsticks, skin on
- oil for misting or cooking spray

**Directions:**
1. Beat together egg and buttermilk in shallow dish.
2. In a second shallow dish, combine the flour, panko crumbs, salt, and pepper.
3. Sprinkle chicken legs with additional salt and pepper to taste.
4. Dip legs in buttermilk mixture, then roll in panko mixture, pressing in crumbs to make coating stick. Mist with oil or cooking spray.
5. Spray air fryer basket with cooking spray.
6. Cook drumsticks at 360°F for 10minutes. Turn pieces over and cook an additional 10minutes.
7. Turn pieces to check for browning. If you have any white spots that haven't begun to brown, spritz them with oil or cooking spray. Continue cooking for 5 more minutes or until crust is golden brown and juices run clear. Larger, meatier drumsticks will take longer to cook than small ones.

# Sweet Nutty Chicken Breasts

Servings:4
Cooking Time: 30 Minutes
**Ingredients:**
- 2 chicken breasts, halved lengthwise
- ¼ cup honey mustard
- ¼ cup chopped pecans
- 1 tbsp olive oil
- 1 tbsp parsley, chopped

**Directions:**
1. Preheat air fryer to 350ºF. Brush chicken breasts with honey mustard and olive oil on all sides. Place the pecans in a bowl. Add and coat the chicken breasts. Place the breasts in the greased frying basket and Air Fry for 25 minutes, turning once. Let chill onto a serving plate for 5 minutes. Sprinkle with parsley and serve.

# Spiced Mexican Stir-fried Chicken

Servings: 4
Cooking Time: 30 Minutes
**Ingredients:**
- 1 lb chicken breasts, cubed
- 2 green onions, chopped
- 1 red bell pepper, chopped
- 1 jalapeño pepper, minced
- 2 tsp olive oil
- 2/3 cup canned black beans
- ½ cup salsa
- 2 tsp Mexican chili powder

**Directions:**
1. Preheat air fryer to 400°F. Combine the chicken, green onions, bell pepper, jalapeño, and olive oil in a bowl. Transfer to a bowl to the frying basket and Air Fry for 10 minutes, stirring once during cooking. When done, stir in the black beans, salsa, and chili powder. Air Fry for 7-10 minutes or until cooked through. Serve.

# Chicken Souvlaki Gyros

Servings: 4
Cooking Time: 18 Minutes
**Ingredients:**
- ¼ cup extra-virgin olive oil
- 1 clove garlic, crushed
- 1 tablespoon Italian seasoning
- ½ teaspoon paprika
- ½ lemon, sliced
- ¼ teaspoon salt
- 1 pound boneless, skinless chicken breasts
- 4 whole-grain pita breads
- 1 cup shredded lettuce
- ½ cup chopped tomatoes
- ¼ cup chopped red onion
- ¼ cup cucumber yogurt sauce

**Directions:**
1. In a large resealable plastic bag, combine the olive oil, garlic, Italian seasoning, paprika, lemon, and salt. Add the chicken to the bag and secure shut. Vigorously shake until all the ingredients are combined. Set in the fridge for 2 hours to marinate.
2. When ready to cook, preheat the air fryer to 360°F.
3. Liberally spray the air fryer basket with olive oil mist. Remove the chicken from the bag and discard the leftover marinade. Place the chicken into the air fryer basket, allowing enough room between the chicken breasts to flip.
4. Cook for 10 minutes, flip, and cook another 8 minutes.
5. Remove the chicken from the air fryer basket when it has cooked (or the internal temperature of the chicken reaches 165°F). Let rest 5 minutes. Then thinly slice the chicken into strips.
6. Assemble the gyros by placing the pita bread on a flat surface and topping with chicken, lettuce, tomatoes, onion, and a drizzle of yogurt sauce.
7. Serve warm.

# Daadi Chicken Salad

Servings: 2
Cooking Time: 30 Minutes
**Ingredients:**
- ½ cup chopped golden raisins
- 1 Granny Smith apple, grated
- 2 chicken breasts
- Salt and pepper to taste
- ¾ cup mayonnaise
- 1 tbsp lime juice
- 1 tsp curry powder
- ½ sliced avocado
- 1 scallion, minced
- 2 tbsp chopped pecans

- 1 tsp poppy seeds

**Directions:**

1. Preheat air fryer at 350ºF. Sprinkle chicken breasts with salt and pepper, place them in the greased frying basket, and Air Fry for 8-10 minutes, tossing once. Let rest for 5 minutes before cutting. In a salad bowl, combine chopped chicken, mayonnaise, lime juice, curry powder, raisins, apple, avocado, scallion, and pecans. Let sit covered in the fridge until ready to eat. Before serve sprinkled with the poppy seeds.

# Chicken Rochambeau

Servings: 4
Cooking Time: 20 Minutes
**Ingredients:**

- 1 tablespoon butter
- 4 chicken tenders, cut in half crosswise
- salt and pepper
- ¼ cup flour
- oil for misting
- 4 slices ham, ¼- to ⅜-inches thick and large enough to cover an English muffin
- 2 English muffins, split
- Sauce
- 2 tablespoons butter
- ½ cup chopped green onions
- ½ cup chopped mushrooms
- 2 tablespoons flour
- 1 cup chicken broth
- ¼ teaspoon garlic powder
- 1½ teaspoons Worcestershire sauce

**Directions:**

1. Place 1 tablespoon of butter in air fryer baking pan and cook at 390°F for 2minutes to melt.
2. Sprinkle chicken tenders with salt and pepper to taste, then roll in the ¼ cup of flour.
3. Place chicken in baking pan, turning pieces to coat with melted butter.
4. Cook at 390°F for 5minutes. Turn chicken pieces over, and spray tops lightly with olive oil. Cook 5minutes longer or until juices run clear. The chicken will not brown.
5. While chicken is cooking, make the sauce: In a medium saucepan, melt the 2 tablespoons of butter.

6. Add onions and mushrooms and sauté until tender, about 3minutes.
7. Stir in the flour. Gradually add broth, stirring constantly until you have a smooth gravy.
8. Add garlic powder and Worcestershire sauce and simmer on low heat until sauce thickens, about 5minutes.
9. When chicken is cooked, remove baking pan from air fryer and set aside.
10. Place ham slices directly into air fryer basket and cook at 390°F for 5minutes or until hot and beginning to sizzle a little. Remove and set aside on top of the chicken for now.
11. Place the English muffin halves in air fryer basket and cook at 390°F for 1 minute.
12. Open air fryer and place a ham slice on top of each English muffin half. Stack 2 pieces of chicken on top of each ham slice. Cook at 390°F for 1 to 2minutes to heat through.
13. Place each English muffin stack on a serving plate and top with plenty of sauce.

# Yogurt-marinated Chicken Legs

Servings: 4
Cooking Time: 50 Minutes
**Ingredients:**

- 1 cup Greek yogurt
- 1 tbsp Dijon mustard
- 1 tsp smoked paprika
- 1 tbsp crushed red pepper
- 1 tsp garlic powder
- 1 tsp dried oregano
- 1 tsp dried thyme
- 1 teaspoon ground cumin
- ¼ cup lemon juice
- Salt and pepper to taste
- 1 ½ lb chicken legs
- 3 tbsp butter, melted

**Directions:**

1. Combine all ingredients, except chicken and butter, in a bowl. Fold in chicken legs and toss until coated. Let sit covered in the fridge for 60 minutes up to overnight.
2. Preheat air fryer at 375ºF. Shake excess marinade from chicken; place them in the greased frying basket and Air Fry for 18 minutes, brush melted butter and flip once. Let chill for 5 minutes before serving.

# Bacon & Chicken Flatbread

Servings: 2
Cooking Time: 35 Minutes
**Ingredients:**

- 1 flatbread dough
- 1 chicken breast, cubed
- 1 cup breadcrumbs
- 2 eggs, beaten
- Salt and pepper to taste
- 2 tsp dry rosemary
- 1 tsp fajita seasoning
- 1 tsp onion powder
- 3 bacon strips
- ½ tbsp ranch sauce

**Directions:**

1. Preheat air fryer to 360°F. Place the breadcrumbs, onion powder, rosemary, salt, and pepper in a mixing bowl. Coat the chicken with the mixture, dip into the beaten eggs, then roll again into the dry ingredients. Arrange the coated chicken pieces on one side of the greased frying basket. On the other side of the basket, lay the bacon strips. Air Fry for 6 minutes. Turn the bacon pieces over and flip the chicken and cook for another 6 minutes.

2. Roll the flatbread out and spread the ranch sauce all over the surface. Top with the bacon and chicken and sprinkle with fajita seasoning. Close the bread to contain the filling and place it in the air fryer. Cook for 10 minutes, flipping the flatbread once until golden brown. Let it cool for a few minutes. Then slice and serve.

# Crispy Duck With Cherry Sauce

Servings: 2
Cooking Time: 33 Minutes
**Ingredients:**

- 1 whole duck (up to 5 pounds), split in half, back and rib bones removed
- 1 teaspoon olive oil
- salt and freshly ground black pepper
- Cherry Sauce:
- 1 tablespoon butter
- 1 shallot, minced
- ½ cup sherry
- ¾ cup cherry preserves 1 cup chicken stock
- 1 teaspoon white wine vinegar
- 1 teaspoon fresh thyme leaves
- salt and freshly ground black pepper

**Directions:**

1. Preheat the air fryer to 400°F.

2. Trim some of the fat from the duck. Rub olive oil on the duck and season with salt and pepper. Place the duck halves in the air fryer basket, breast side up and facing the center of the basket.

3. Air-fry the duck for 20 minutes. Turn the duck over and air-fry for another 6 minutes.

4. While duck is air-frying, make the cherry sauce. Melt the butter in a large sauté pan. Add the shallot and sauté until it is just starting to brown – about 2 to 3 minutes. Add the sherry and deglaze the pan by scraping up any brown bits from the bottom of the pan. Simmer the liquid for a few minutes, until it has reduced by half. Add the cherry preserves, chicken stock and white wine vinegar. Whisk well to combine all the ingredients. Simmer the sauce until it thickens and coats the back of a spoon – about 5 to 7 minutes. Season with salt and pepper and stir in the fresh thyme leaves.

5. When the air fryer timer goes off, spoon some cherry sauce over the duck and continue to air-fry at 400°F for 4 more minutes. Then, turn the duck halves back over so that the breast side is facing up. Spoon more cherry sauce over the top of the duck, covering the skin completely. Air-fry for 3 more minutes and then remove the duck to a plate to rest for a few minutes.

6. Serve the duck in halves, or cut each piece in half again for a smaller serving. Spoon any additional sauce over the duck or serve it on the side.

# Fish And Seafood Recipes

## Oyster Shrimp With Fried Rice

Servings: 4
Cooking Time: 40 Minutes
Ingredients:

- 1 lb peeled shrimp, deveined
- 1 shallot, chopped
- 2 garlic cloves, minced
- 1 tbsp olive oil
- 1 tbsp butter
- 2 eggs, beaten
- 2 cups cooked rice
- 1 cup baby peas
- 2 tbsp fish sauce
- 1 tbsp oyster sauce

Directions:

1. Preheat the air fryer to 370°F. Combine the shrimp, shallot, garlic, and olive oil in a cake pan. Put the cake pan in the air fryer and Bake the shrimp for 5-7 minutes, stirring once until shrimp are no pinker. Remove into a bowl, and set aside. Put the butter in the hot cake pan to melt. Add the eggs and return to the fryer. Bake for 4-6 minutes, stirring once until the eggs are set. Remove the eggs from the pan and set aside.

2. Add the rice, peas, oyster sauce, and fish sauce to the pan and return it to the fryer. Bake for 12-15 minutes, stirring once halfway through. Pour in the shrimp and eggs and stir. Cook for 2-3 more minutes until everything is hot.

## Lobster Tails With Lemon Garlic Butter

Servings: 2
Cooking Time: 5 Minutes
Ingredients:

- 4 ounces unsalted butter
- 1 tablespoon finely chopped lemon zest
- 1 clove garlic, thinly sliced
- 2 (6-ounce) lobster tails
- salt and freshly ground black pepper
- ½ cup white wine
- ½ lemon, sliced
- vegetable oil

Directions:

1. Start by making the lemon garlic butter. Combine the butter, lemon zest and garlic in a small saucepan. Melt and simmer the butter on the stovetop over the lowest possible heat while you prepare the lobster tails.

2. Prepare the lobster tails by cutting down the middle of the top of the shell. Crack the bottom shell by squeezing the sides of the lobster together so that you can access the lobster meat inside. Pull the lobster tail up out of the shell, but leave it attached at the base of the tail. Lay the lobster meat on top of the shell and season with salt and freshly ground black pepper. Pour a little of the lemon garlic butter on top of the lobster meat and transfer the lobster to the refrigerator so that the butter solidifies a little.

3. Pour the white wine into the air fryer drawer and add the lemon slices. Preheat the air fryer to 400°F for 5 minutes.

4. Transfer the lobster tails to the air fryer basket. Air-fry at 370° for 5 minutes, brushing more butter on halfway through cooking. (Add a minute or two if your lobster tail is more than 6-ounces.) Remove and serve with more butter for dipping or drizzling.

## Firecracker Popcorn Shrimp

Servings: 6
Cooking Time: 8 Minutes
Ingredients:

- ½ cup all-purpose flour
- 2 teaspoons ground paprika
- 1 teaspoon garlic powder
- ½ teaspoon black pepper
- ¼ teaspoon salt
- 2 eggs, whisked
- 1½ cups panko breadcrumbs
- 1 pound small shrimp, peeled and deveined

Directions:

1. Preheat the air fryer to 360°F.

2. In a medium bowl, place the flour and mix in the paprika, garlic powder, pepper, and salt.

3. In a shallow dish, place the eggs.

4. In a third dish, place the breadcrumbs.

5. Assemble the shrimp by covering them in the flour, then dipping them into the egg, and then coating them with the breadcrumbs. Repeat until all the shrimp are covered in the breading.

6. Liberally spray the metal trivet that fits in the air fryer basket with olive oil mist. Place the shrimp onto the trivet, leaving space between the shrimp to flip. Cook for 4 minutes, flip the shrimp, and cook another 4 minutes. Repeat until all the shrimp are cooked.

7. Serve warm with desired dipping sauce.


## Sea Bass With Fruit Salsa

Servings: 4
Cooking Time: 30 Minutes
**Ingredients:**
- 3 halved nectarines, pitted
- 4 sea bass fillets
- 2 tsp olive oil
- 3 plums, halved and pitted
- 1 cup red grapes
- 1 tbsp lemon juice
- 1 tbsp honey
- ½ tsp dried thyme


**Directions:**
1. Preheat air fryer to 390°F. Lay the sea bass fillets in the frying basket, then spritz olive oil over the top. Air Fry for 4 minutes. Take the basket out of the fryer and add the nectarines and plums. Pour the grapes over, spritz with lemon juice and honey, then add a pinch of thyme. Put the basket back into the fryer and Bake for 5-9 minutes. The fish should flake when finished, and the fruits should be soft. Serve hot.


## Sriracha Salmon Melt Sandwiches

Servings: 4
Cooking Time: 20 Minutes
**Ingredients:**
- 2 tbsp butter, softened
- 2 cans pink salmon
- 2 English muffins
- 1/3 cup mayonnaise
- 2 tbsp Dijon mustard
- 1 tbsp fresh lemon juice
- 1/3 cup chopped celery
- ½ tsp sriracha sauce
- 4 slices tomato
- 4 slices Swiss cheese


**Directions:**
1. Preheat the air fryer to 370°F. Split the English muffins with a fork and spread butter on the 4 halves. Put the halves in the basket and Bake for 3-5 minutes, or until toasted. Remove and set aside. Combine the salmon, mayonnaise, mustard, lemon juice, celery, and sriracha in a bowl. Divide among the English muffin halves. Top each sandwich with tomato and cheese and put in the frying basket. Bake for 4-6 minutes or until the cheese is melted and starts to brown. Serve hot.


## Quick Shrimp Scampi

Servings: 2
Cooking Time: 5 Minutes
**Ingredients:**
- 16 to 20 raw large shrimp, peeled, deveined and tails removed
- ½ cup white wine
- freshly ground black pepper
- ¼ cup + 1 tablespoon butter, divided
- 1 clove garlic, sliced
- 1 teaspoon olive oil
- salt, to taste
- juice of ½ lemon, to taste
- ¼ cup chopped fresh parsley


**Directions:**
1. Start by marinating the shrimp in the white wine and freshly ground black pepper for at least 30 minutes, or as long as 2 hours in the refrigerator.

2. Preheat the air fryer to 400°F.

3. Melt ¼ cup of butter in a small saucepan on the stovetop. Add the garlic and let the butter simmer, but be sure to not let it burn.

4. Pour the shrimp and marinade into the air fryer, letting the marinade drain through to the bottom drawer. Drizzle the olive oil on the shrimp and season well with salt. Air-fry at 400°F for 3 minutes. Turn the shrimp over (don't shake the

basket because the marinade will splash around) and pour the garlic butter over the shrimp. Air-fry for another 2 minutes.

5. Remove the shrimp from the air fryer basket and transfer them to a bowl. Squeeze lemon juice over all the shrimp and toss with the chopped parsley and remaining tablespoon of butter. Season to taste with salt and serve immediately.

# Cheese & Crab Stuffed Mushrooms

Servings: 2
Cooking Time: 30 Minutes
**Ingredients:**

- 6 oz lump crabmeat, shells discarded
- 6 oz mascarpone cheese, softened
- 2 jalapeño peppers, minced
- ¼ cup diced red onions
- 2 tsp grated Parmesan cheese
- 2 portobello mushroom caps
- 2 tbsp butter, divided
- ½ tsp prepared horseradish
- ¼ tsp Worcestershire sauce
- ¼ tsp smoked paprika
- Salt and pepper to taste
- ¼ cup bread crumbs

**Directions:**

1. Melt 1 tbsp of butter in a skillet over heat for 30 seconds. Add in onion and cook for 3 minutes until tender. Stir in mascarpone cheese, Parmesan cheese, horseradish, jalapeño peppers, Worcestershire sauce, paprika, salt and pepper and cook for 2 minutes until smooth. Fold in crabmeat. Spoon mixture into mushroom caps. Set aside.

2. Preheat air fryer at 350ºF. Microwave the remaining butter until melted. Stir in breadcrumbs. Scatter over stuffed mushrooms. Place mushrooms in the greased frying basket and Bake for 8 minutes. Serve immediately.

# Horseradish-crusted Salmon Fillets

Servings:3
Cooking Time: 8 Minutes
**Ingredients:**

- ½ cup Fresh bread crumbs (see the headnote)
- 4 tablespoons (¼ cup/½ stick) Butter, melted and cooled
- ¼ cup Jarred prepared white horseradish
- Vegetable oil spray

- 4 6-ounce skin-on salmon fillets (for more information, see here)

**Directions:**

1. Preheat the air fryer to 400°F.

2. Mix the bread crumbs, butter, and horseradish in a bowl until well combined.

3. Take the basket out of the machine. Generously spray the skin side of each fillet. Pick them up one by one with a nonstick-safe spatula and set them in the basket skin side down with as much air space between them as possible. Divide the bread-crumb mixture between the fillets, coating the top of each fillet with an even layer. Generously coat the bread-crumb mixture with vegetable oil spray.

4. Return the basket to the machine and air-fry undisturbed for 8 minutes, or until the topping has lightly browned and the fish is firm but not hard.

5. Use a nonstick-safe spatula to transfer the salmon fillets to serving plates. Cool for 5 minutes before serving. Because of the butter in the topping, it will stay very hot for quite a while. Take care, especially if you're serving these fillets to children.

# King Prawns Al Ajillo

Servings: 4
Cooking Time: 15 Minutes
**Ingredients:**

- 1 ¼ lb peeled king prawns, deveined
- ½ cup grated Parmesan
- 1 tbsp olive oil
- 1 tbsp lemon juice
- ½ tsp garlic powder
- 2 garlic cloves, minced

**Directions:**

1. Preheat the air fryer to 350°F. In a large bowl, add the prawns and sprinkle with olive oil, lemon juice, and garlic powder. Toss in the minced garlic and Parmesan, then toss to coat. Put the prawns in the frying basket and Air Fry for 10-15 minutes or until the prawns cook through. Shake the basket once while cooking. Serve immediately.

# Salty German-style Shrimp Pancakes

Servings: 4
Cooking Time: 15 Minutes
**Ingredients:**

- 1 tbsp butter
- 3 eggs, beaten
- ½ cup flour
- ½ cup milk
- ⅛ tsp salt
- 1 cup salsa
- 1 cup cooked shrimp, minced
- 2 tbsp cilantro, chopped

**Directions:**

1. Preheat air fryer to 390°F. Mix the eggs, flour, milk, and salt in a bowl until frothy. Pour the batter into a greased baking pan and place in the air fryer. Bake for 15 minutes or until the pancake is puffed and golden. Flip the pancake onto a plate. Mix salsa, shrimp, and cilantro. Top the pancake and serve.

# Saucy Shrimp

Servings: 4
Cooking Time: 30 Minutes
**Ingredients:**

- 1 lb peeled shrimp, deveined
- ½ cup grated coconut
- ¼ cup bread crumbs
- ¼ cup flour
- ¼ tsp smoked paprika
- Salt and pepper to taste
- 1 egg
- 2 tbsp maple syrup
- ½ tsp rice vinegar
- 1 tbsp hot sauce
- ⅛ tsp red pepper flakes
- ¼ cup orange juice
- 1 tsp cornstarch
- ½ cup banana ketchup
- 1 lemon, sliced

**Directions:**

1. Preheat air fryer to 350°F. Combine coconut, bread crumbs, flour, paprika, black pepper, and salt in a bowl. In a separate bowl, whisk egg and 1 teaspoon water. Dip one shrimp into the egg bowl and shake off excess drips. Dip the shrimp in the bread crumb mixture and coat it completely. Continue the process for all of the shrimp. Arrange the shrimp on the greased frying basket. Air Fry for 5 minutes, then use tongs to flip the shrimp. Cook for another 2-3 minutes.

2. To make the sauce, add maple syrup, banana ketchup, hot sauce, vinegar, and red pepper flakes in a small saucepan over medium heat. Make a slurry in a small bowl with orange juice and cornstarch. Stir in slurry and continue stirring. Bring the sauce to a boil and cook for 5 minutes. When the sauce begins to thicken, remove from heat and allow to sit for 5 minutes. Serve shrimp warm along with sauce and lemon slices on the side.

# Rich Salmon Burgers With Broccoli Slaw

Servings: 4
Cooking Time: 25 Minutes
**Ingredients:**

- 1 lb salmon fillets
- 1 egg
- ¼ cup dill, chopped
- 1 cup bread crumbs
- Salt to taste
- ½ tsp cayenne pepper
- 1 lime, zested
- 1 tsp fish sauce
- 4 buns
- 3 cups chopped broccoli
- ½ cup shredded carrots
- ¼ cup sunflower seeds
- 2 garlic cloves, minced
- 1 cup Greek yogurt

**Directions:**

1. Preheat air fryer to 360°F. Blitz the salmon fillets in your food processor until they are finely chopped. Remove to a large bowl and add egg, dill, bread crumbs, salt, and cayenne. Stir to combine. Form the mixture into 4 patties. Put them into the frying basket and Bake for 10 minutes, flipping once. Combine broccoli, carrots, sunflower seeds,

garlic, salt, lime, fish sauce, and Greek yogurt in a bowl. Serve the salmon burgers onto buns with broccoli slaw. Enjoy!

## Potato Chip-crusted Cod

Servings: 2
Cooking Time: 20 Minutes
**Ingredients:**
- ½ cup crushed potato chips
- 1 tsp chopped tarragon
- 1/8 tsp salt
- 1 tsp cayenne powder
- 1 tbsp Dijon mustard
- ¼ cup buttermilk
- 1 tsp lemon juice
- 1 tbsp butter, melted
- 2 cod fillets

**Directions:**
1. Preheat air fryer at 350ºF. Mix all ingredients in a bowl. Press potato chip mixture evenly across tops of cod. Place cod fillets in the greased frying basket and Air Fry for 10 minutes until the fish is opaque and flakes easily with a fork. Serve immediately.

## Mediterranean Salmon Burgers

Servings: 4
Cooking Time: 30 Minutes
**Ingredients:**
- 1 lb salmon fillets
- 1 scallion, diced
- 4 tbsp mayonnaise
- 1 egg
- 1 tsp capers, drained
- Salt and pepper to taste
- ¼ tsp paprika
- 1 lemon, zested
- 1 lemon, sliced
- 1 tbsp chopped dill
- ¼ cup bread crumbs
- 4 buns, toasted
- 4 tsp whole-grain mustard
- 4 lettuce leaves
- 1 small tomato, sliced

**Directions:**
1. Preheat air fryer to 400°F. Divide salmon in half. Cut one of the halves into chunks and transfer the chunks to the food processor. Also, add scallion, 2 tablespoons mayonnaise, egg, capers, dill, salt, pepper, paprika, and lemon zest. Pulse to puree. Dice the rest of the salmon into ¼-inch chunks. Combine chunks and puree along with bread crumbs in a large bowl. Shape the fish into 4 patties and transfer to the frying basket. Air Fry for 5 minutes, then flip the patties. Air Fry for another 5 to 7 minutes. Place the patties each on a bun along with 1 teaspoon mustard, mayonnaise, lettuce, lemon slices, and a slice of tomato. Serve and enjoy.

## Teriyaki Salmon

Servings: 4
Cooking Time: 20 Minutes
**Ingredients:**
- ¼ cup raw honey
- 4 garlic cloves, minced
- 1 tbsp olive oil
- ½ tsp salt
- ½ tsp soy sauce
- ¼ tsp blackening seasoning
- 4 salmon fillets

**Directions:**
1. Preheat air fryer to 380°F. Combine together the honey, garlic, olive oil, soy sauce, blackening seasoning and salt in a bowl. Put the salmon in a single layer on the greased frying basket. Brush the top of each fillet with the honey-garlic mixture. Roast for 10-12 minutes. Serve and enjoy!

# Fried Scallops

Servings:3
Cooking Time: 6 Minutes
**Ingredients:**
- ½ cup All-purpose flour or tapioca flour
- 1 Large egg(s), well beaten
- 2 cups Corn flake crumbs (gluten-free, if a concern)
- Up to 2 teaspoons Cayenne
- 1 teaspoon Celery seeds
- 1 teaspoon Table salt
- 1 pound Sea scallops
- Vegetable oil spray

**Directions:**
1. Preheat the air fryer to 400°F.
2. Set up and fill three shallow soup plates or small pie plates on your counter: one for the flour; one for the beaten egg(s); and one for the corn flake crumbs, stirred with the cayenne, celery seeds, and salt until well combined.
3. One by one, dip a scallop in the flour, turning it every way to coat it thoroughly. Gently shake off any excess flour, then dip the scallop in the egg(s), turning it again to coat all sides. Let any excess egg slip back into the rest, then set the scallop in the corn flake mixture. Turn it several times, pressing gently to get an even coating on the scallop all around. Generously coat the scallop with vegetable oil spray, then set it aside on a cutting board. Coat the remaining scallops in the same way.
4. Set the scallops in the basket with as much air space between them as possible. They should not touch. Air-fry undisturbed for 6 minutes, or until lightly browned and firm.
5. Use kitchen tongs to gently transfer the scallops to a wire rack. Cool for only a minute or two before serving.

# Catalan Sardines With Romesco Sauce

Servings:2
Cooking Time: 15 Minutes
**Ingredients:**
- 2 cans skinless, boneless sardines in oil, drained
- ½ cup warmed romesco sauce
- ½ cup bread crumbs

**Directions:**

1. Preheat air fryer to 350ºF. In a shallow dish, add bread crumbs. Roll in sardines to coat. Place sardines in the greased frying basket and Air Fry for 6 minutes, turning once. Serve with romesco sauce.

# Herby Prawn & Zucchini Bake

Servings: 4
Cooking Time: 30 Minutes
**Ingredients:**
- 1 ¼ lb prawns, peeled and deveined
- 2 zucchini, sliced
- 2 tbsp butter, melted
- ½ tsp garlic salt
- 1 ½ tsp dried oregano
- ⅛ tsp red pepper flakes
- ½ lemon, juiced
- 1 tbsp chopped mint
- 1 tbsp chopped dill

**Directions:**

1. Preheat air fryer to 350°F. Combine prawns, zucchini, butter, garlic salt, oregano, and pepper flakes in a large bowl. Toss to coat. Put the prawns and zucchini in the greased frying basket and Air Fry for about 6-8 minutes, shaking the basket once until the zucchini is golden and the shrimp are cooked. Remove the shrimp to a serving plate and cover with foil. Serve hot topped with lemon juice, mint, and dill. Enjoy!

# Spiced Shrimp Empanadas

Servings: 5
Cooking Time: 30 Minutes
**Ingredients:**
- ½ lb peeled and deveined shrimp, chopped
- 2 tbsp diced red bell peppers
- 1 shallot, minced
- 1 scallion, chopped
- 2 garlic cloves, minced
- 2 tbsp chopped cilantro
- ½ tbsp lemon juice
- ¼ tsp sweet paprika
- ⅛ tsp salt

- ⅛ tsp red pepper flakes
- ¼ tsp ground nutmeg
- 1 large egg, beaten
- 10 empanada discs

**Directions:**

1. Combine all ingredients, except the egg and empanada discs, in a bowl. Toss to coat. Beat the 1 egg with 1 tsp of water in a small bowl until blended. Set aside.

2. On your work board, place one empanada disc. Add 2 tbsp of shrimp mixture in the middle. Brush the edges of the disc with the egg mixture. Fold the disc in half and seal the edges. Crimp with a fork by pressing around the edges. Brush the tops with the egg mixture. Preheat air fryer to 380°F. Put the empanadas in the greased frying basket and Air Fry for 9 minutes, flipping once until golden and crispy. Serve hot.

## Shrimp Patties

Servings: 4
Cooking Time: 10 Minutes
**Ingredients:**

- ½ pound shelled and deveined raw shrimp
- ¼ cup chopped red bell pepper
- ¼ cup chopped green onion
- ¼ cup chopped celery
- 2 cups cooked sushi rice
- ½ teaspoon garlic powder
- ½ teaspoon Old Bay Seasoning
- ½ teaspoon salt
- 2 teaspoons Worcestershire sauce
- ½ cup plain breadcrumbs
- oil for misting or cooking spray

**Directions:**

1. Finely chop the shrimp. You can do this in a food processor, but it takes only a few pulses. Be careful not to overprocess into mush.

2. Place shrimp in a large bowl and add all other ingredients except the breadcrumbs and oil. Stir until well combined.

3. Preheat air fryer to 390°F.

4. Shape shrimp mixture into 8 patties, no more than ½-inch thick. Roll patties in breadcrumbs and mist with oil or cooking spray.

5. Place 4 shrimp patties in air fryer basket and cook at 390°F for 10 minutes, until shrimp cooks through and outside is crispy.

6. Repeat step 5 to cook remaining shrimp patties.

## Crab Cakes

Servings: 2
Cooking Time: 10 Minutes
**Ingredients:**

- 1 teaspoon butter
- ⅓ cup finely diced onion
- ⅓ cup finely diced celery
- ¼ cup mayonnaise
- 1 teaspoon Dijon mustard
- 1 egg
- pinch ground cayenne pepper
- 1 teaspoon salt
- freshly ground black pepper
- 16 ounces lump crabmeat
- ½ cup + 2 tablespoons panko breadcrumbs, divided

**Directions:**

1. Melt the butter in a skillet over medium heat. Sauté the onion and celery until it starts to soften, but not brown – about 4 minutes. Transfer the cooked vegetables to a large bowl. Add the mayonnaise, Dijon mustard, egg, cayenne pepper, salt and freshly ground black pepper to the bowl. Gently fold in the lump crabmeat and 2 tablespoons of panko breadcrumbs. Stir carefully so you don't break up all the crab pieces.

2. Preheat the air fryer to 400°F.

3. Place the remaining panko breadcrumbs in a shallow dish. Divide the crab mixture into 4 portions and shape each portion into a round patty. Dredge the crab patties in the breadcrumbs, coating both sides as well as the edges with the crumbs.

4. Air-fry the crab cakes for 5 minutes. Using a flat spatula, gently turn the cakes over and air-fry for another 5 minutes. Serve the crab cakes with tartar sauce or cocktail sauce, or dress it up with the suggestion below.

# Tuna Nuggets In Hoisin Sauce

Servings: 4
Cooking Time: 7 Minutes
**Ingredients:**

- ½ cup hoisin sauce
- 2 tablespoons rice wine vinegar
- 2 teaspoons sesame oil
- 1 teaspoon garlic powder
- 2 teaspoons dried lemongrass
- ¼ teaspoon red pepper flakes
- ½ small onion, quartered and thinly sliced
- 8 ounces fresh tuna, cut into 1-inch cubes
- cooking spray
- 3 cups cooked jasmine rice

**Directions:**

1. Mix the hoisin sauce, vinegar, sesame oil, and seasonings together.
2. Stir in the onions and tuna nuggets.
3. Spray air fryer baking pan with nonstick spray and pour in tuna mixture.
4. Cook at 390°F for 3minutes. Stir gently.
5. Cook 2minutes and stir again, checking for doneness. Tuna should be barely cooked through, just beginning to flake and still very moist. If necessary, continue cooking and stirring in 1-minute intervals until done.
6. Serve warm over hot jasmine rice.

# Smoked Paprika Cod Goujons

Servings: 2
Cooking Time: 30 Minutes
**Ingredients:**

- 1 cod fillet, cut into chunks
- 2 eggs, beaten
- ¼ cup breadcrumbs
- ¼ cup rice flour
- 1 lemon, juiced
- ½ tbsp garlic powder
- 1 tsp smoked paprika
- Salt and pepper to taste

**Directions:**

1. Preheat air fryer to 350°F. In a bowl, stir the beaten eggs and lemon juice thoroughly. Dip the cod chunks in the mixture. In another bowl, mix the bread crumbs, rice flour, garlic powder, smoked paprika, salt, and pepper.
2. Coat the cod with the crumb mixture. Transfer the coated cod to the greased frying basket. Air Fry for 14-16 minutes until the fish goujons are cooked through and their crust is golden, brown, and delicious. Toss the basket two or three times during the cooking time. Serve.

# Fish Sticks With Tartar Sauce

Servings: 2
Cooking Time: 6 Minutes
**Ingredients:**

- 12 ounces cod or flounder
- ½ cup flour
- ½ teaspoon paprika
- 1 teaspoon salt
- lots of freshly ground black pepper
- 2 eggs, lightly beaten
- 1½ cups panko breadcrumbs
- 1 teaspoon salt
- vegetable oil
- Tartar Sauce:
- ¼ cup mayonnaise
- 2 teaspoons lemon juice
- 2 tablespoons finely chopped sweet pickles
- salt and freshly ground black pepper

**Directions:**

1. Cut the fish into ¾-inch wide sticks or strips. Set up a dredging station. Combine the flour, paprika, salt and pepper in a shallow dish. Beat the eggs lightly in a second shallow dish. Finally, mix the breadcrumbs and salt in a third shallow dish. Coat the fish sticks by dipping the fish into the flour, then the egg and finally the breadcrumbs, coating on all sides in each step and pressing the crumbs firmly onto the fish. Place the finished sticks on a plate or baking sheet while you finish all the sticks.
2. Preheat the air fryer to 400°F.
3. Spray the fish sticks with the oil and spray or brush the bottom of the air fryer basket. Place the fish into the basket and air-fry at 400°F for 4 minutes, turn the fish sticks over, and air-fry for another 2 minutes.
4. While the fish is cooking, mix the tartar sauce ingredients together.

5. Serve the fish sticks warm with the tartar sauce and some French fries on the side.

# Blackened Red Snapper

Servings: 4
Cooking Time: 8 Minutes
**Ingredients:**

- 1½ teaspoons black pepper
- ¼ teaspoon thyme
- ¼ teaspoon garlic powder
- ⅛ teaspoon cayenne pepper
- 1 teaspoon olive oil
- 4 4-ounce red snapper fillet portions, skin on
- 4 thin slices lemon
- cooking spray

**Directions:**

1. Mix the spices and oil together to make a paste. Rub into both sides of the fish.
2. Spray air fryer basket with nonstick cooking spray and lay snapper steaks in basket, skin-side down.
3. Place a lemon slice on each piece of fish.
4. Cook at 390°F for 8 minutes. The fish will not flake when done, but it should be white through the center.

# Sinaloa Fish Fajitas

Servings: 4
Cooking Time: 30 Minutes
**Ingredients:**

- 1 lemon, thinly sliced
- 16 oz red snapper filets
- 1 tbsp olive oil
- 1 tbsp cayenne pepper
- ½ tsp salt
- 2 cups shredded coleslaw
- 1 carrot, shredded
- 2 tbsp orange juice
- ½ cup salsa
- 4 flour tortillas
- ½ cup sour cream
- 2 avocados, sliced

**Directions:**

1. Preheat the air fryer to 350°F. Lay the lemon slices at the bottom of the basket. Drizzle the fillets with olive oil and sprinkle with cayenne pepper and salt. Lay the fillets on top of the lemons and Bake for 6-9 minutes or until the fish easily flakes. While the fish cooks, toss the coleslaw, carrot, orange juice, and salsa in a bowl. When the fish is done, remove it and cover. Toss the lemons. Air Fry the tortillas for 2-3 minutes to warm up. Add the fish to the tortillas and top with a cabbage mix, sour cream, and avocados. Serve and enjoy!

# Basil Crab Cakes With Fresh Salad

Servings:2
Cooking Time: 25 Minutes
**Ingredients:**

- 8 oz lump crabmeat
- 2 tbsp mayonnaise
- ½ tsp Dijon mustard
- ½ tsp lemon juice
- ½ tsp lemon zest
- 2 tsp minced yellow onion
- ¼ tsp prepared horseradish
- ¼ cup flour
- 1 egg white, beaten
- 1 tbsp basil, minced
- 1 tbsp olive oil
- 2 tsp white wine vinegar
- Salt and pepper to taste
- 4 oz arugula
- ½ cup blackberries
- ¼ cup pine nuts
- 2 lemon wedges

**Directions:**

1. Preheat air fryer to 400°F. Combine the crabmeat, mayonnaise, mustard, lemon juice and zest, onion, horseradish, flour, egg white, and basil in a bowl. Form mixture into 4 patties. Place the patties in the lightly greased frying basket and Air Fry for 10 minutes, flipping once. Combine olive oil, vinegar, salt, and pepper in a bowl. Toss in the arugula and share into 2 medium bowls. Add 2 crab cakes to each bowl and scatter with blackberries, pine nuts, and lemon wedges. Serve warm.

# Tuna Patties With Dill Sauce

Servings: 6
Cooking Time: 10 Minutes
**Ingredients:**

- Two 5-ounce cans albacore tuna, drained
- ½ teaspoon garlic powder
- 2 teaspoons dried dill, divided
- ½ teaspoon black pepper
- ½ teaspoon salt, divided
- ¼ cup minced onion
- 1 large egg
- 7 tablespoons mayonnaise, divided
- ¼ cup panko breadcrumbs
- 1 teaspoon fresh lemon juice
- ¼ teaspoon fresh lemon zest
- 6 pieces butterleaf lettuce
- 1 cup diced tomatoes

**Directions:**

1. In a large bowl, mix the tuna with the garlic powder, 1 teaspoon of the dried dill, the black pepper, ¼ teaspoon of the salt, and the onion. Make sure to use the back of a fork to really break up the tuna so there are no large chunks.
2. Mix in the egg and 1 tablespoon of the mayonnaise; then fold in the breadcrumbs so the tuna begins to form a thick batter that holds together.
3. Portion the tuna mixture into 6 equal patties and place on a plate lined with parchment paper in the refrigerator for at least 30 minutes. This will help the patties hold together in the air fryer.
4. When ready to cook, preheat the air fryer to 350°F.
5. Liberally spray the metal trivet that sits inside the air fryer basket with olive oil mist and place the patties onto the trivet.
6. Cook for 5 minutes, flip, and cook another 5 minutes.
7. While the patties are cooking, make the dill sauce by combining the remaining 6 tablespoons of mayonnaise with the remaining 1 teaspoon of dill, the lemon juice, the lemon zest, and the remaining ¼ teaspoon of salt. Set aside.
8. Remove the patties from the air fryer.
9. Place 1 slice of lettuce on a plate and top with the tuna patty and a tomato slice. Repeat to form the remaining servings. Drizzle the dill dressing over the top. Serve immediately.

# Southeast Asian-style Tuna Steaks

Servings: 4
Cooking Time: 20 Minutes
**Ingredients:**

- 1 stalk lemongrass, bent in half
- 4 tuna steaks
- 2 tbsp soy sauce
- 2 tsp sesame oil
- 2 tsp rice wine vinegar
- 1 tsp grated fresh ginger
- ⅛ tsp pepper
- 3 tbsp lemon juice
- 2 tbsp chopped cilantro
- 1 sliced red chili

**Directions:**

1. Preheat air fryer to 390°F. Place the tuna steak on a shallow plate. Mix together soy sauce, sesame oil, rice wine vinegar, and ginger in a small bowl. Pour over the tuna, rubbing the marinade gently into both sides of the fish. Marinate for about 10 minutes. Then sprinkle with pepper. Place the lemongrass in the frying basket and top with tuna steaks. Add the remaining lemon juice and 1 tablespoon of water in the pan below the basket. Bake until the tuna is cooked through, 8-10 minutes. Discard the lemongrass before topping with cilantro and red chili. Serve and enjoy!

# Summer Sea Scallops

Servings: 4
Cooking Time: 30 Minutes
**Ingredients:**

- 1 cup asparagus
- 1 cup peas
- 1 cup chopped broccoli
- 2 tsp olive oil
- ½ tsp dried oregano
- 12 oz sea scallops

**Directions:**

1. Preheat air fryer to 400°F. Add the asparagus, peas, and broccoli to a bowl and mix with olive oil. Put the bowl in the fryer and Air Fry for 4-6 minutes until crispy and soft. Take the veggies out and add the herbs; let sit. Add the scallops to the fryer and Air Fry for 4-5 minutes until the scallops are springy to the touch. Serve immediately with the vegetables. Enjoy!

# Vegetable Side Dishes Recipes

## Sage & Thyme Potatoes

Servings: 4
Cooking Time: 30 Minutes
**Ingredients:**
- 2 red potatoes, peeled and cubed
- ¼ cup olive oil
- 1 tsp dried sage
- ½ tsp dried thyme
- ½ tsp salt
- 2 tbsp grated Parmesan

**Directions:**

1. Preheat air fryer to 360°F. Coat the red potatoes with olive oil, sage, thyme and salt in a bowl. Pour the potatoes into the air frying basket and Roast for 10 minutes. Stir the potatoes and sprinkle the Parmesan over the top. Continue roasting for 8 more minutes. Serve hot.

## Herb Roasted Jicama

Servings: 6
Cooking Time: 25 Minutes
**Ingredients:**
- 1 lb jicama, cut into fries
- ¼ cup olive oil
- Salt and pepper to taste
- 1 garlic clove, minced
- 4 thyme sprigs

**Directions:**

1. Preheat air fryer to 360°F. Coat the jicamas with olive oil, salt, pepper, and garlic in a bowl. Pour the jicama fries into the frying basket and top with the thyme sprigs. Roast for 20 minutes, stirring twice. Remove the rosemary sprigs. Serve and enjoy!

## Roman Artichokes

Servings: 4
Cooking Time: 12 Minutes

**Ingredients:**
- 2 9-ounce box(es) frozen artichoke heart quarters, thawed
- 1½ tablespoons Olive oil
- 2 teaspoons Minced garlic
- 1 teaspoon Table salt
- Up to ½ teaspoon Red pepper flakes

**Directions:**

1. Preheat the air fryer to 400°F.

2. Gently toss the artichoke heart quarters, oil, garlic, salt, and red pepper flakes in a bowl until the quarters are well coated.

3. When the machine is at temperature, scrape the contents of the bowl into the basket. Spread the artichoke heart quarters out into as close to one layer as possible. Air-fry undisturbed for 8 minutes. Gently toss and rearrange the quarters so that any covered or touching parts are now exposed to the air currents, then air-fry undisturbed for 4 minutes more, until very crisp.

4. Gently pour the contents of the basket onto a wire rack. Cool for a few minutes before serving.

## Garlic-parmesan Popcorn

Servings: 2
Cooking Time: 15 Minutes
**Ingredients:**
- 2 tsp grated Parmesan cheese
- ¼ cup popcorn kernels
- 1 tbsp lemon juice
- 1 tsp garlic powder

**Directions:**

1. Preheat air fryer to 400°F. Line the basket with aluminum foil. Put the popcorn kernels in a single layer and Grill for 6-8 minutes until they stop popping. Remove them into a bowl. Drizzle with lemon juice and toss until well coated. Sprinkle with garlic powder and grated Parmesan and toss to coat. Drizzle with more lemon juice. Serve.

# Glazed Carrots

Servings: 4
Cooking Time: 10 Minutes
**Ingredients:**
- 2 teaspoons honey
- 1 teaspoon orange juice
- ½ teaspoon grated orange rind
- ⅛ teaspoon ginger
- 1 pound baby carrots
- 2 teaspoons olive oil
- ¼ teaspoon salt

**Directions:**
1. Combine honey, orange juice, grated rind, and ginger in a small bowl and set aside.
2. Toss the carrots, oil, and salt together to coat well and pour them into the air fryer basket.
3. Cook at 390°F for 5minutes. Shake basket to stir a little and cook for 4 minutes more, until carrots are barely tender.
4. Pour carrots into air fryer baking pan.
5. Stir the honey mixture to combine well, pour glaze over carrots, and stir to coat.
6. Cook at 360°F for 1 minute or just until heated through.

# Hot Okra Wedges

Servings: 2
Cooking Time: 35 Minutes
**Ingredients:**
- 1 cup okra, sliced
- 1 cup breadcrumbs
- 2 eggs, beaten
- A pinch of black pepper
- 1 tsp crushed red peppers
- 2 tsp hot Tabasco sauce

**Directions:**
1. Preheat air fryer to 350°F. Place the eggs and Tabasco sauce in a bowl and stir thoroughly; set aside. In a separate mixing bowl, combine the breadcrumbs, crushed red peppers, and pepper. Dip the okra into the beaten eggs, then coat in the crumb mixture. Lay the okra pieces on the greased frying basket. Air Fry for 14-16 minutes, shaking the basket several times during cooking. When ready, the okra will be crispy and golden brown. Serve.

# Asparagus Wrapped In Pancetta

Servings: 4
Cooking Time: 30 Minutes
**Ingredients:**
- 20 asparagus trimmed
- Salt and pepper pepper
- 4 pancetta slices
- 1 tbsp fresh sage, chopped

**Directions:**
1. Sprinkle the asparagus with fresh sage, salt and pepper. Toss to coat. Make 4 bundles of 5 spears by wrapping the center of the bunch with one slice of pancetta.
2. Preheat air fryer to 400°F. Put the bundles in the greased frying basket and Air Fry for 8-10 minutes or until the pancetta is brown and the asparagus are starting to char on the edges. Serve immediately.

# Broccoli Au Gratin

Servings: 2
Cooking Time: 25 Minutes
**Ingredients:**
- 2 cups broccoli florets, chopped
- 6 tbsp grated Gruyère cheese
- 1 tbsp grated Pecorino cheese
- ½ tbsp olive oil
- 1 tbsp flour
- 1/3 cup milk
- ½ tsp ground coriander
- Salt and black pepper
- 2 tbsp panko bread crumbs

**Directions:**
1. Whisk the olive oil, flour, milk, coriander, salt, and pepper in a bowl. Incorporate broccoli, Gruyere cheese, panko bread crumbs, and Pecorino cheese until well combined. Pour in a greased baking dish.
2. Preheat air fryer to 330°F. Put the baking dish into the frying basket. Bake until the broccoli is crisp-tender and the top is golden, or about 12-15 minutes. Serve warm.

# Chicken Eggrolls

Servings: 10
Cooking Time: 17 Minutes
**Ingredients:**

- 1 tablespoon vegetable oil
- ¼ cup chopped onion
- 1 clove garlic, minced
- 1 cup shredded carrot
- ½ cup thinly sliced celery
- 2 cups cooked chicken
- 2 cups shredded white cabbage
- ½ cup teriyaki sauce
- 20 egg roll wrappers
- 1 egg, whisked
- 1 tablespoon water

**Directions:**

1. Preheat the air fryer to 390°F.
2. In a large skillet, heat the oil over medium-high heat. Add in the onion and sauté for 1 minute. Add in the garlic and sauté for 30 seconds. Add in the carrot and celery and cook for 2 minutes. Add in the chicken, cabbage, and teriyaki sauce. Allow the mixture to cook for 1 minute, stirring to combine. Remove from the heat.
3. In a small bowl, whisk together the egg and water for brushing the edges.
4. Lay the eggroll wrappers out at an angle. Place ¼ cup filling in the center. Fold the bottom corner up first and then fold in the corners; roll up to complete eggroll.
5. Place the eggrolls in the air fryer basket, spray with cooking spray, and cook for 8 minutes, turn over, and cook another 2 to 4 minutes.

# Sage Hasselback Potatoes

Servings: 4
Cooking Time: 45 Minutes
**Ingredients:**

- 1 lb fingerling potatoes
- 1 tbsp olive oil
- 1 tbsp butter
- 1tsp dried sage
- Salt and pepper to taste

**Directions:**

1. Preheat the air fryer to 400°F. Rinse the potatoes dry, then set them on a work surface and put two chopsticks lengthwise on either side of each so you won't cut all the way through. Make vertical, crosswise cuts in the potato, about ⅛ inch apart. Repeat with the remaining potatoes. Combine the olive oil and butter in a bowl and microwave for 30 seconds or until melted. Stir in the sage, salt, and pepper. Put the potatoes in a large bowl and drizzle with the olive oil mixture. Toss to coat, then put the potatoes in the fryer and Air Fry for 22-27 minutes, rearranging them after 10-12 minutes. Cook until the potatoes are tender. Serve hot and enjoy!

# Crispy, Cheesy Leeks

Servings: 4
Cooking Time: 15 Minutes
**Ingredients:**

- 2 Medium leek(s), about 9 ounces each
- Olive oil spray
- ¼ cup Seasoned Italian-style dried bread crumbs (gluten-free, if a concern)
- ¼ cup (about ¾ ounce) Finely grated Parmesan cheese
- 2 tablespoons Olive oil

**Directions:**

1. Preheat the air fryer to 350°F .
2. Trim off the root end of the leek(s) as well as the dark green top(s), leaving about a 5-inch usable section. Split the leek section(s) in half lengthwise. Set the leek halves cut side up on your work surface. Pull out and remove in one piece the semicircles that make up the inner structure of the leek, about halfway down. Set the removed "inside" next to the outer leek "shells" on your cutting board. Generously coat them all on all sides (particularly the "bottoms") with olive oil spray.
3. Set the leeks and their insides cut side up in the basket with as much air space between them as possible. Air-fry undisturbed for 12 minutes.
4. Meanwhile, mix the bread crumbs, cheese, and olive oil in a small bowl until well combined.
5. After 12 minutes in the air fryer, sprinkle this mixture inside the leek shells and on top of the leek insides. Increase the machine's temperature to 375°F (or 380°F or 390°F, if one of these is the closest setting). Air-fry undisturbed for 3 minutes, or until the topping is lightly browned.
6. Use a nonstick-safe spatula to transfer the leeks to a serving platter. Cool for a few minutes before serving warm.

# Tomato Candy

Servings: 12
Cooking Time: 120 Minutes
**Ingredients:**
- 6 Small Roma or plum tomatoes, halved lengthwise
- 1½ teaspoons Coarse sea salt or kosher salt

**Directions:**
1. Before you turn the machine on, set the tomatoes cut side up in a single layer in the basket (or the basket attachment). They can touch each other, but try to leave at least a fraction of an inch between them (depending, of course, on the size of the basket or basket attachment). Sprinkle the cut sides of the tomatoes with the salt.
2. Set the machine to cook at 225°F (or 230°F, if that's the closest setting). Put the basket in the machine and air-fry for 2 hours, or until the tomatoes are dry but pliable, with a little moisture down in their centers.
3. Remove the basket from the machine and cool the tomatoes in it for 10 minutes before gently transferring them to a plate for serving, or to a shallow dish that you can cover and store in the refrigerator for up to 1 week.

# Balsamic Beet Chips

Servings: 4
Cooking Time: 40 Minutes
**Ingredients:**
- ½ tsp balsamic vinegar
- 4 beets, peeled and sliced
- 1 garlic clove, minced
- 2 tbsp chopped mint
- Salt and pepper to taste
- 3 tbsp olive oil

**Directions:**
1. Preheat air fryer to 380°F. Coat all ingredients in a bowl, except balsamic vinegar. Pour the beet mixture into the frying basket and Roast for 25-30 minutes, stirring once. Serve, drizzled with vinegar and enjoy!

# Sea Salt Radishes

Servings: 4

Cooking Time: 25 Minutes
**Ingredients:**
- 1 lb radishes
- 2 tbsp olive oil
- ½ tsp sea salt
- ½ tsp garlic powder

**Directions:**
1. Preheat air fryer to 360°F. Toss the radishes with olive oil, garlic powder, and salt in a bowl. Pour them into the air fryer. Air Fry for 18 minutes, turning once. Serve.

# Mouth-watering Provençal Mushrooms

Servings: 4
Cooking Time: 35 Minutes
**Ingredients:**
- 2 lb mushrooms, quartered
- 2-3 tbsp olive oil
- ½ tsp garlic powder
- 2 tsp herbs de Provence
- 2 tbsp dry white wine

**Directions:**
1. Preheat air fryer to 320°F. Beat together the olive oil, garlic powder, herbs de Provence, and white wine in a bowl. Add the mushrooms and toss gently to coat. Spoon the mixture onto the frying basket and Bake for 16-18 minutes, stirring twice. Serve hot and enjoy!

# Horseradish Potato Mash

Servings: 4
Cooking Time: 50 Minutes
**Ingredients:**
- 1 lb baby potatoes
- 1 tbsp horseradish sauce
- ½ cup vegetable broth
- ½ tsp sea salt
- 3 tbsp butter
- 2 garlic cloves, minced
- 2 tsp chili powder

**Directions:**

1. Preheat the air fryer to 400°F. Combine the potatoes, broth, and salt in a cake pan, then cover with foil and put it in the frying basket. Bake for 20 minutes, stirring once until they are almost tender. Drain and place them on a baking sheet. With the bottom of a glass, smash the potatoes, but don't break them apart. Put a small saucepan on the stove and mix butter, garlic, chili powder, and horseradish sauce. Melt the butter over low heat, then brush over the potatoes. Put as many as will fit in the basket in a single layer, butter-side down. Brush the tops with more of the butter mix, and Bake for 12-17 minutes, turning once until they're crisp. Keep the cooked potatoes warm in the oven at 250°F while air frying the rest of the potatoes.

## Simple Zucchini Ribbons

Servings:4
Cooking Time: 15 Minutes
**Ingredients:**

- 2 zucchini
- 2 tsp butter, melted
- ¼ tsp garlic powder
- ¼ tsp chili flakes
- 8 cherry tomatoes, halved
- Salt and pepper to taste

**Directions:**

1. Preheat air fryer to 275°F. Cut the zucchini into ribbons with a vegetable peeler. Mix them with butter, garlic, chili flakes, salt, and pepper in a bowl. Transfer to the frying basket and Air Fry for 2 minutes. Toss and add the cherry tomatoes. Cook for another 2 minutes. Serve.

## Sweet Potato Fries

Servings: 4
Cooking Time: 30 Minutes
**Ingredients:**

- 2 pounds sweet potatoes
- 1 teaspoon dried marjoram
- 2 teaspoons olive oil
- sea salt

**Directions:**

1. Peel and cut the potatoes into ¼-inch sticks, 4 to 5 inches long.
2. In a sealable plastic bag or bowl with lid, toss sweet potatoes with marjoram and olive oil. Rub seasonings in to coat well.
3. Pour sweet potatoes into air fryer basket and cook at 390°F for approximately 30 minutes, until cooked through with some brown spots on edges.
4. Season to taste with sea salt.

## Mom´s Potatoes Au Gratin

Servings: 4
Cooking Time: 50 Minutes
**Ingredients:**

- 4 Yukon Gold potatoes, peeled
- 1cup shredded cheddar cheese
- 2 tbsp grated Parmesan cheese
- 2 garlic cloves, minced
- 1/3 cup heavy cream
- 1/3 cup whole milk
- ½ tsp dried marjoram
- Salt and pepper to taste

**Directions:**

1. Preheat the air fryer to 350°F. Spray a 7-inch round pan thoroughly with cooking oil. Cut the potatoes into ⅛-inch-thick slices and layer the potatoes inside the pan along with cheddar cheese and garlic. Mix the cream, milk, marjoram, salt, and pepper in a bowl, then slowly pour the mix over the potatoes. Sprinkle with Parmesan and put the pan in the fryer. Bake for 25-35 minutes or until the potatoes are tender, the sauce is bubbling, and the top is golden. Serve warm.

# Pecorino Dill Muffins

Servings:4
Cooking Time: 25 Minutes
**Ingredients:**

- ¼ cup grated Pecorino cheese
- 1 cup flour
- 1 tsp dried dill
- ⅛ tsp salt
- ¼ tsp onion powder
- 2 tsp baking powder
- 1 egg
- ¼ cup Greek yogurt

**Directions:**

1. Preheat air fryer to 350°F. In a bowl, combine dry the ingredients. Set aside. In another bowl, whisk the wet ingredients. Add the wet ingredients to the dry ingredients and combine until blended.
2. Transfer the batter to 6 silicone muffin cups lightly greased with olive oil. Place muffin cups in the frying basket and Bake for 12 minutes. Serve right away.

# Broccoli Tots

Servings: 24
Cooking Time: 10 Minutes
**Ingredients:**

- 2 cups broccoli florets (about ½ pound broccoli crowns)
- 1 egg, beaten
- ⅛ teaspoon onion powder
- ¼ teaspoon salt
- ⅛ teaspoon pepper
- 2 tablespoons grated Parmesan cheese
- ¼ cup panko breadcrumbs
- oil for misting

**Directions:**

1. Steam broccoli for 2minutes. Rinse in cold water, drain well, and chop finely.
2. In a large bowl, mix broccoli with all other ingredients except the oil.
3. Scoop out small portions of mixture and shape into 24 tots. Lay them on a cookie sheet or wax paper as you work.
4. Spray tots with oil and place in air fryer basket in single layer.

5. Cook at 390°F for 5minutes. Shake basket and spray with oil again. Cook 5minutes longer or until browned and crispy.

# Polenta

Servings: 4
Cooking Time: 15 Minutes
**Ingredients:**

- 1 pound polenta
- ¼ cup flour
- oil for misting or cooking spray

**Directions:**

1. Cut polenta into ½-inch slices.
2. Dip slices in flour to coat well. Spray both sides with oil or cooking spray.
3. Cook at 390°F for 5minutes. Turn polenta and spray both sides again with oil.
4. Cook 10 more minutes or until brown and crispy.

# Sticky Broccoli Florets

Servings: 4
Cooking Time: 20 Minutes
**Ingredients:**

- 4 cups broccoli florets
- 2 tbsp olive oil
- ½ tsp salt
- ½ cup grapefruit juice
- 1 tbsp raw honey
- 4-6 grapefruit wedges

**Directions:**

1. Preheat air fryer to 360°F. Add the broccoli, olive oil, salt, grapefruit juice, and honey to a bowl. Toss the broccoli in the liquid until well coated. Pour the broccoli mixture into the frying basket and Roast for 12 minutes, stirring once. Serve with grapefruit wedges.

# Chili-oiled Brussels Sprouts

Servings: 4
Cooking Time: 30 Minutes
**Ingredients:**

- 1 cup Brussels sprouts, quartered
- 1 tsp olive oil
- 1 tsp chili oil
- Salt and pepper to taste

**Directions:**

1. Preheat air fryer to 350°F. Coat the Brussels sprouts with olive oil, chili oil, salt, and black pepper in a bowl. Transfer to the frying basket. Bake for 20 minutes, shaking the basket several times throughout cooking until the sprouts are crispy, browned on the outside, and juicy inside. Serve and enjoy!

# Mexican-style Roasted Corn

Servings: 3
Cooking Time: 14 Minutes
**Ingredients:**

- 3 tablespoons Butter, melted and cooled
- 2 teaspoons Minced garlic
- ¾ teaspoon Ground cumin
- Up to ¾ teaspoon Red pepper flakes
- ¼ teaspoon Table salt
- 3 Cold 4-inch lengths husked and de-silked corn on the cob
- Minced fresh cilantro leaves
- Crumbled queso fresco

**Directions:**

1. Preheat the air fryer to 400°F.
2. Mix the melted butter, garlic, cumin, red pepper flakes, and salt in a large zip-closed plastic bag. Add the cold corn pieces, seal the bag, and massage the butter mixture into the surface of the corn.
3. When the machine is at temperature, take the pieces of corn out of the plastic bag and put them in the basket with as much air space between the pieces as possible. Air-fry undisturbed for 14 minutes, until golden brown and maybe even charred in a few small spots.

4. Use kitchen tongs to gently transfer the pieces of corn to a serving platter. Sprinkle each piece with the cilantro and queso fresco. Serve warm.

# Hush Puppies

Servings: 8
Cooking Time: 11 Minutes
**Ingredients:**

- ½ cup Whole or low-fat milk (not fat-free)
- 1½ tablespoons Butter
- ½ cup plus 1 tablespoon, plus more All-purpose flour
- ½ cup plus 1 tablespoon Yellow cornmeal
- 2 teaspoons Granulated white sugar
- 2 teaspoons Baking powder
- ¾ teaspoon Baking soda
- ¾ teaspoon Table salt
- ¼ teaspoon Onion powder
- 3 tablespoons (or 1 medium egg, well beaten) Pasteurized egg substitute, such as Egg Beaters
- Vegetable oil spray

**Directions:**

1. Heat the milk and butter in a small saucepan set over medium heat just until the butter melts and the milk is steamy. Do not simmer or boil.
2. Meanwhile, whisk the flour, cornmeal, sugar, baking powder, baking soda, salt, and onion powder in a large bowl until the mixture is a uniform color.
3. Stir the hot milk mixture into the flour mixture to form a dough. Set aside to cool for 5 minutes.
4. Mix the egg substitute or egg into the dough to make a thick, smooth batter. Cover and refrigerate for at least 1 hour or up to 4 hours.
5. Preheat the air fryer to 350°F .
6. Lightly flour your clean, dry hands. Roll 2 tablespoons of the batter into a ball between your floured palms. Set aside, flour your hands again if necessary, and continue making more balls with the remaining batter.
7. Coat the balls all over with the vegetable oil spray. Line the machine's basket (or basket attachment) with a piece of parchment paper. Set the balls on the parchment paper with as much air space between them as possible. Air-fry for 9 minutes, or until lightly browned and set.
8. Use kitchen tongs to gently transfer the hush puppies to a wire rack. Cool for at least 5 minutes before serving. Or

cool to room temperature, about 45 minutes, and store in a sealed container at room temperature for up to 2 days. To crisp the hush puppies again, put them in a 350°F air fryer for 2 minutes. (There's no need for parchment paper in the machine during reheating.)

## Fried Eggplant Balls

Servings: 4
Cooking Time: 40 Minutes
**Ingredients:**
- 1 medium eggplant (about 1 pound)
- olive oil
- salt and freshly ground black pepper
- 1 cup grated Parmesan cheese
- 2 cups fresh breadcrumbs
- 2 tablespoons chopped fresh parsley
- 2 tablespoons chopped fresh basil
- 1 clove garlic, minced
- 1 egg, lightly beaten
- ½ cup fine dried breadcrumbs

**Directions:**
1. Preheat the air fryer to 400°F.
2. Quarter the eggplant by cutting it in half both lengthwise and horizontally. Make a few slashes in the flesh of the eggplant but not through the skin. Brush the cut surface of the eggplant generously with olive oil and transfer to the air fryer basket, cut side up. Air-fry for 10 minutes. Turn the eggplant quarters cut side down and air-fry for another 15 minutes or until the eggplant is soft all the way through. You may need to rotate the pieces in the air fryer so that they cook evenly. Transfer the eggplant to a cutting board to cool.
3. Place the Parmesan cheese, the fresh breadcrumbs, fresh herbs, garlic and egg in a food processor. Scoop the flesh out of the eggplant, discarding the skin and any pieces that are tough. You should have about 1 to 1½ cups of eggplant. Add the eggplant to the food processor and process everything together until smooth. Season with salt and pepper. Refrigerate the mixture for at least 30 minutes.
4. Place the dried breadcrumbs into a shallow dish or onto a plate. Scoop heaping tablespoons of the eggplant mixture into the dried breadcrumbs. Roll the dollops of eggplant in the breadcrumbs and then shape into small balls. You should have 16 to 18 eggplant balls at the end. Refrigerate until you are ready to air-fry.

5. Preheat the air fryer to 350°F.
6. Spray the eggplant balls and the air fryer basket with olive oil. Air-fry the eggplant balls for 15 minutes, rotating the balls during the cooking process to brown evenly.

## Shoestring Butternut Squash Fries

Servings: 3
Cooking Time: 16 Minutes
**Ingredients:**
- 1 pound 2 ounces Spiralized butternut squash strands
- Vegetable oil spray
- To taste Coarse sea salt or kosher salt

**Directions:**
1. Preheat the air fryer to 375°F .
2. Place the spiralized squash in a big bowl. Coat the strands with vegetable oil spray, toss well, coat again, and toss several times to make sure all the strands have been oiled.
3. When the machine is at temperature, pour the strands into the basket and spread them out into as even a layer as possible. Air-fry for 16 minutes, tossing and rearranging the strands every 4 minutes, or until they're lightly browned and crisp.
4. Pour the contents of the basket into a serving bowl, add salt to taste, and toss well before serving hot.

## Cheese Sage Cauliflower

Servings:4
Cooking Time: 25 Minutes
**Ingredients:**
- 1 head cauliflower, cut into florets
- 3 tbsp butter, melted
- 2 tbsp grated asiago cheese
- 2 tsp dried sage
- ½ tsp garlic powder
- ¼ tsp salt

**Directions:**
1. Preheat air fryer to 350°F. Mix all ingredients in a bowl. Add cauliflower mixture to the frying basket and Air Fry for 6 minutes, shaking once. Serve immediately.

## Roasted Broccoli And Red Bean Salad

Servings: 3
Cooking Time: 14 Minutes
**Ingredients:**
- 3 cups (about 1 pound) 1- to 1½-inch fresh broccoli florets (not frozen)
- 1½ tablespoons Olive oil spray
- 1¼ cups Canned red kidney beans, drained and rinsed
- 3 tablespoons Minced yellow or white onion
- 2 tablespoons plus 1 teaspoon Red wine vinegar
- ¾ teaspoon Dried oregano
- ¼ teaspoon Table salt
- ¼ teaspoon Ground black pepper

**Directions:**

1. Preheat the air fryer to 375°F .
2. Put the broccoli florets in a big bowl, coat them generously with olive oil spray, then toss to coat all surfaces, even down into the crannies, spraying them a couple of times more.
3. Pour the florets into the basket, spreading them into as close to one layer as you can. Air-fry for 12 minutes, tossing and rearranging the florets twice so that any touching or covered parts are eventually exposed to the air currents, until light browned but still a bit firm. (If the machine is at 360°F, you may need to add 2 minutes to the cooking time.)
4. Dump the contents of the basket onto a large cutting board. Cool for a minute or two, then chop the florets into small bits. Scrape these into a bowl and add the kidney beans, onion, vinegar, oregano, salt, and pepper. Toss well and serve warm or at room temperature.

# Vegetarians Recipes

## Thai Peanut Veggie Burgers

Servings: 6
Cooking Time: 14 Minutes
**Ingredients:**
- One 15.5-ounce can cannellini beans
- 1 teaspoon minced garlic
- ¼ cup chopped onion
- 1 Thai chili pepper, sliced
- 2 tablespoons natural peanut butter
- ½ teaspoon black pepper
- ½ teaspoon salt
- ⅓ cup all-purpose flour (optional)
- ½ cup cooked quinoa
- 1 large carrot, grated
- 1 cup shredded red cabbage
- ¼ cup peanut dressing
- ¼ cup chopped cilantro
- 6 Hawaiian rolls
- 6 butterleaf lettuce leaves

**Directions:**

1. Preheat the air fryer to 350°F.
2. To a blender or food processor fitted with a metal blade, add the beans, garlic, onion, chili pepper, peanut butter, pepper, and salt. Pulse for 5 to 10 seconds. Do not over process. The mixture should be coarse, not smooth.
3. Remove from the blender or food processor and spoon into a large bowl. Mix in the cooked quinoa and carrots. At this point, the mixture should begin to hold together to form small patties. If the dough appears to be too sticky (meaning you likely processed a little too long), add the flour to hold the patties together.
4. Using a large spoon, form 8 equal patties out of the batter.
5. Liberally spray a metal trivet with olive oil spray and set in the air fryer basket. Place the patties into the basket, leaving enough space to be able to turn them with a spatula.
6. Cook for 7 minutes, flip, and cook another 7 minutes.
7. Remove from the heat and repeat with additional patties.
8. To serve, place the red cabbage in a bowl and toss with peanut dressing and cilantro. Place the veggie burger on a bun, and top with a slice of lettuce and cabbage slaw.

# Creamy Broccoli & Mushroom Casserole

Servings:4
Cooking Time: 30 Minutes
**Ingredients:**

- 4 cups broccoli florets, chopped
- 1 cup crushed cheddar cheese crisps
- ¼ cup diced onion
- ¼ tsp dried thyme
- ¼ tsp dried marjoram
- ¼ tsp dried oregano
- ½ cup diced mushrooms
- 1 egg
- 2 tbsp sour cream
- ¼ cup mayonnaise
- Salt and pepper to taste

**Directions:**

1. Preheat air fryer to 350ºF. Combine all ingredients, except for the cheese crisps, in a bowl. Spoon mixture into a round cake pan. Place cake pan in the frying basket and Bake for 14 minutes. Let sit for 10 minutes. Distribute crushed cheddar cheese crisps over the top and serve.

# Bell Pepper & Lentil Tacos

Servings: 2
Cooking Time: 40 Minutes
**Ingredients:**

- 2 corn tortilla shells
- ½ cup cooked lentils
- ½ white onion, sliced
- ½ red pepper, sliced
- ½ green pepper, sliced
- ½ yellow pepper, sliced
- ½ cup shredded mozzarella
- ½ tsp Tabasco sauce

**Directions:**

1. Preheat air fryer to 320°F. Sprinkle half of the mozzarella cheese over one of the tortillas, then top with lentils, Tabasco sauce, onion, and peppers. Scatter the remaining mozzarella cheese, cover with the other tortilla and place in the frying basket. Bake for 6 minutes, flipping halfway through cooking. Serve and enjoy!

# Vegetable Couscous

Servings: 4
Cooking Time: 10 Minutes
**Ingredients:**

- 4 ounces white mushrooms, sliced
- ½ medium green bell pepper, julienned
- 1 cup cubed zucchini
- ¼ small onion, slivered
- 1 stalk celery, thinly sliced
- ¼ teaspoon ground coriander
- ¼ teaspoon ground cumin
- salt and pepper
- 1 tablespoon olive oil
- Couscous
- ¾ cup uncooked couscous
- 1 cup vegetable broth or water
- ½ teaspoon salt (omit if using salted broth)

**Directions:**

1. Combine all vegetables in large bowl. Sprinkle with coriander, cumin, and salt and pepper to taste. Stir well, add olive oil, and stir again to coat vegetables evenly.

2. Place vegetables in air fryer basket and cook at 390°F for 5minutes. Stir and cook for 5 more minutes, until tender.

3. While vegetables are cooking, prepare the couscous: Place broth or water and salt in large saucepan. Heat to boiling, stir in couscous, cover, and remove from heat.

4. Let couscous sit for 5minutes, stir in cooked vegetables, and serve hot.

# Crispy Avocados With Pico De Gallo

Servings:2
Cooking Time: 15 Minutes
**Ingredients:**

- 1 cup diced tomatoes
- 1 tbsp lime juice
- 1 tsp lime zest
- 2 tbsp chopped cilantro
- 1 serrano chiles, minced
- 2 cloves garlic, minced
- 1 tbsp diced white onions
- ½ tsp salt
- 2 avocados, halved and pitted
- 4 tbsp cheddar shreds

**Directions:**

1. Preheat air fryer to 350ºF. Combine all ingredients, except for avocados and cheddar cheese, in a bowl and let chill covered in the fridge. Place avocado halves, cut sides-up, in the frying basket, scatter cheese shreds over top of avocado halves, and Air Fry for 4 minutes. Top with pico de gallo and serve.

# Spicy Sesame Tempeh Slaw With Peanut Dressing

Servings: 2
Cooking Time: 8 Minutes
**Ingredients:**

- 2 cups hot water
- 1 teaspoon salt
- 8 ounces tempeh, sliced into 1-inch-long pieces
- 2 tablespoons low-sodium soy sauce
- 2 tablespoons rice vinegar
- 1 tablespoon filtered water
- 2 teaspoons sesame oil
- ½ teaspoon fresh ginger
- 1 clove garlic, minced
- ¼ teaspoon black pepper
- ½ jalapeño, sliced
- 4 cups cabbage slaw
- 4 tablespoons Peanut Dressing (see the following recipe)
- 2 tablespoons fresh chopped cilantro
- 2 tablespoons chopped peanuts

**Directions:**

1. Mix the hot water with the salt and pour over the tempeh in a glass bowl. Stir and cover with a towel for 10 minutes.
2. Discard the water and leave the tempeh in the bowl.
3. In a medium bowl, mix the soy sauce, rice vinegar, filtered water, sesame oil, ginger, garlic, pepper, and jalapeño. Pour over the tempeh and cover with a towel. Place in the refrigerator to marinate for at least 2 hours.
4. Preheat the air fryer to 370°F. Remove the tempeh from the bowl and discard the remaining marinade.
5. Liberally spray the metal trivet that goes into the air fryer basket and place the tempeh on top of the trivet.
6. Cook for 4 minutes, flip, and cook another 4 minutes.
7. In a large bowl, mix the cabbage slaw with the Peanut Dressing and toss in the cilantro and chopped peanuts.

8. Portion onto 4 plates and place the cooked tempeh on top when cooking completes. Serve immediately.

# Zucchini Tacos

Servings: 3
Cooking Time: 20 Minutes
**Ingredients:**

- 1 small zucchini, sliced
- 1 yellow onion, sliced
- ¼ tsp garlic powder
- Salt and pepper to taste
- 1 can refried beans
- 6 corn tortillas, warm
- 1 cup guacamole
- 1 tbsp cilantro, chopped

**Directions:**

1. Preheat air fryer to 390°F. Place the zucchini and onion in the greased frying basket. Spray with more oil and sprinkle with garlic, salt, and pepper to taste. Roast for 6 minutes. Remove, shake, or stir, then cook for another 6 minutes, until the veggies are golden and tender.
2. In a pan, heat the refried beans over low heat. Stir often. When warm enough, remove from heat and set aside. Place a corn tortilla on a plate and fill it with beans, roasted vegetables, and guacamole. Top with cilantro to serve.

# Thyme Lentil Patties

Servings: 2
Cooking Time: 35 Minutes
**Ingredients:**

- ½ cup grated American cheese
- 1 cup cooked lentils
- ¼ tsp dried thyme
- 2 eggs, beaten
- Salt and pepper to taste
- 1 cup bread crumbs

**Directions:**

1. Preheat air fryer to 350°F. Put the eggs, lentils, and cheese in a bowl and mix to combine. Stir in half the bread crumbs, thyme, salt, and pepper. Form the mixture into 2 patties and coat them in the remaining bread crumbs. Transfer to the greased frying basket. Air Fry for 14-16 minutes until brown, flipping once. Serve.

# Sweet Roasted Carrots

Servings: 4
Cooking Time: 25 Minutes
**Ingredients:**

- 6 carrots, cut into ½-inch pieces
- 2 tbsp butter, melted
- 2 tbsp parsley, chopped
- 1 tsp honey

**Directions:**

1. Preheat air fryer to 390°F. Add carrots to a baking pan and pour over butter, honey, and 2-3 tbsp of water. Mix well. Transfer the carrots to the greased frying basket and Roast for 12 minutes, shaking the basket once. Sprinkle with parsley and serve warm.

# Thyme Meatless Patties

Servings: 3
Cooking Time: 25 Minutes
**Ingredients:**

- ½ cup oat flour
- 1 tsp allspice
- ½ tsp ground thyme
- 1 tsp maple syrup
- ½ tsp liquid smoke
- 1 tsp balsamic vinegar

**Directions:**

1. Preheat air fryer to 400°F. Mix the oat flour, allspice, thyme, maple syrup, liquid smoke, balsamic vinegar, and 2 tbsp of water in a bowl. Make 6 patties out of the mixture. Place them onto a parchment paper and flatten them to ½-inch thick. Grease the patties with cooking spray. Grill for 12 minutes until crispy, turning once. Serve warm.

# Vegan Buddha Bowls(2)

Servings:4
Cooking Time: 20 Minutes
**Ingredients:**

- 1 carrot, peeled and julienned
- ½ onion, sliced into half-moons

- ¼ cup apple cider vinegar
- ½ tsp ground ginger
- ⅛ tsp cayenne pepper
- 1 parsnip, diced
- 1 tsp avocado oil
- 4 oz extra-firm tofu, cubed
- ½ tsp five-spice powder
- ½ tsp chili powder
- 2 tsp fresh lime zest
- 1 cup fresh arugula
- ½ cup cooked quinoa
- 2 tbsp canned kidney beans
- 2 tbsp canned sweetcorn
- 1 avocado, diced
- 2 tbsp pine nuts

**Directions:**

1. Preheat air fryer to 350°F. Combine carrot, vinegar, ginger, and cayenne in a bowl. In another bowl, combine onion, parsnip, and avocado oil. In a third bowl, mix the tofu, five-spice powder, and chili powder.

2. Place the onion mixture in the greased basket. Air Fry for 6 minutes. Stir in tofu mixture and cook for 8 more minutes. Mix in lime zest. Divide arugula, cooked quinoa, kidney beans, sweetcorn, drained carrots, avocado, pine nuts, and tofu mixture between 2 bowls. Serve.

# Roasted Vegetable Thai Green Curry

Servings: 4
Cooking Time: 16 Minutes
**Ingredients:**

- 1 (13-ounce) can coconut milk
- 3 tablespoons green curry paste
- 1 tablespoon soy sauce*
- 1 tablespoon rice wine vinegar
- 1 teaspoon sugar
- 1 teaspoon minced fresh ginger
- ½ onion, chopped
- 3 carrots, sliced
- 1 red bell pepper, chopped
- olive oil
- 10 stalks of asparagus, cut into 2-inch pieces
- 3 cups broccoli florets
- basmati rice for serving

- fresh cilantro
- crushed red pepper flakes (optional)

**Directions:**

1. Combine the coconut milk, green curry paste, soy sauce, rice wine vinegar, sugar and ginger in a medium saucepan and bring to a boil on the stovetop. Reduce the heat and simmer for 20 minutes while you cook the vegetables. Set aside.

2. Preheat the air fryer to 400°F.

3. Toss the onion, carrots, and red pepper together with a little olive oil and transfer the vegetables to the air fryer basket. Air-fry at 400°F for 10 minutes, shaking the basket a few times during the cooking process. Add the asparagus and broccoli florets and air-fry for an additional 6 minutes, again shaking the basket for even cooking.

4. When the vegetables are cooked to your liking, toss them with the green curry sauce and serve in bowls over basmati rice. Garnish with fresh chopped cilantro and crushed red pepper flakes.


# Quinoa Burgers With Feta Cheese And Dill

Servings: 6
Cooking Time: 10 Minutes
**Ingredients:**

- 1 cup quinoa (red, white or multi-colored)
- 1½ cups water
- 1 teaspoon salt
- freshly ground black pepper
- 1½ cups rolled oats
- 3 eggs, lightly beaten
- ¼ cup minced white onion
- ½ cup crumbled feta cheese
- ¼ cup chopped fresh dill
- salt and freshly ground black pepper
- vegetable or canola oil, in a spray bottle
- whole-wheat hamburger buns (or gluten-free hamburger buns*)
- arugula
- tomato, sliced
- red onion, sliced
- mayonnaise

**Directions:**

1. Make the quinoa: Rinse the quinoa in cold water in a saucepan, swirling it with your hand until any dry husks rise to the surface. Drain the quinoa as well as you can and then put the saucepan on the stovetop to dry and toast the quinoa. Turn the heat to medium-high and shake the pan regularly until you see the quinoa moving easily and can hear the seeds moving in the pan, indicating that they are dry. Add the water, salt and pepper. Bring the liquid to a boil and then reduce the heat to low or medium-low. You should see just a few bubbles, not a boil. Cover with a lid, leaving it askew and simmer for 20 minutes. Turn the heat off and fluff the quinoa with a fork. If there's any liquid left in the bottom of the pot, place it back on the burner for another 3 minutes or so. Spread the cooked quinoa out on a sheet pan to cool.

2. Combine the room temperature quinoa in a large bowl with the oats, eggs, onion, cheese and dill. Season with salt and pepper and mix well (remember that feta cheese is salty). Shape the mixture into 6 patties with flat sides (so they fit more easily into the air fryer). Add a little water or a few more rolled oats if necessary to get the mixture to be the right consistency to make patties.

3. Preheat the air-fryer to 400°F.

4. Spray both sides of the patties generously with oil and transfer them to the air fryer basket in one layer (you will probably have to cook these burgers in batches, depending on the size of your air fryer). Air-fry each batch at 400°F for 10 minutes, flipping the burgers over halfway through the cooking time.

5. Build your burger on the whole-wheat hamburger buns with arugula, tomato, red onion and mayonnaise.


# Tandoori Paneer Naan Pizza

Servings: 4
Cooking Time: 10 Minutes
**Ingredients:**

- 6 tablespoons plain Greek yogurt, divided
- 1¼ teaspoons garam marsala, divided
- ½ teaspoon turmeric, divided
- ¼ teaspoon garlic powder
- ½ teaspoon paprika, divided
- ½ teaspoon black pepper, divided
- 3 ounces paneer, cut into small cubes
- 1 tablespoon extra-virgin olive oil
- 2 teaspoons minced garlic
- 4 cups baby spinach

- 2 tablespoons marinara sauce
- ¼ teaspoon salt
- 2 plain naan breads (approximately 6 inches in diameter)
- ½ cup shredded part-skim mozzarella cheese

**Directions:**

1. Preheat the air fryer to 350°F.
2. In a small bowl, mix 2 tablespoons of the yogurt, ½ teaspoon of the garam marsala, ¼ teaspoon of the turmeric, the garlic powder, ¼ teaspoon of the paprika, and ¼ teaspoon of the black pepper. Toss the paneer cubes in the mixture and let marinate for at least an hour.
3. Meanwhile, in a pan, heat the olive oil over medium heat. Add in the minced garlic and sauté for 1 minute. Stir in the spinach and begin to cook until it wilts. Add in the remaining 4 tablespoons of yogurt and the marinara sauce. Stir in the remaining ¾ teaspoon of garam masala, the remaining ¼ teaspoon of turmeric, the remaining ¼ teaspoon of paprika, the remaining ¼ teaspoon of black pepper, and the salt. Let simmer a minute or two, and then remove from the heat.
4. Equally divide the spinach mixture amongst the two naan breads. Place 1½ ounces of the marinated paneer on each naan.
5. Liberally spray the air fryer basket with olive oil mist.
6. Use a spatula to pick up one naan and place it in the air fryer basket.
7. Cook for 4 minutes, open the basket and sprinkle ¼ cup of mozzarella cheese on top, and cook another 4 minutes.
8. Remove from the air fryer and repeat with the remaining naan.
9. Serve warm.

# Pinto Bean Casserole

Servings: 2
Cooking Time: 15 Minutes
**Ingredients:**

- 1 can pinto beans
- ¼ cup tomato sauce
- 2 tbsp cornstarch
- 2 garlic cloves, minced
- ½ tsp dried oregano
- ½ tsp cumin
- 1 tsp smoked paprika
- Salt and pepper to taste

**Directions:**

1. Preheat air fryer to 390°F. Stir the beans, tomato sauce, cornstarch, garlic, oregano, cumin, smoked paprika, salt, and pepper in a bowl until combined. Pour the bean mix into a greased baking pan. Bake in the fryer for 4 minutes. Remove, stir, and Bake for 4 minutes or until the mix is thick and heated through. Serve hot.

# Broccoli Cheddar Stuffed Potatoes

Servings: 2
Cooking Time: 42 Minutes
**Ingredients:**

- 2 large russet potatoes, scrubbed
- 1 tablespoon olive oil
- salt and freshly ground black pepper
- 2 tablespoons butter
- ¼ cup sour cream
- 3 tablespoons half-and-half (or milk)
- 1¼ cups grated Cheddar cheese, divided
- ¾ teaspoon salt
- freshly ground black pepper
- 1 cup frozen baby broccoli florets, thawed and drained

**Directions:**

1. Preheat the air fryer to 400°F.
2. Rub the potatoes all over with olive oil and season generously with salt and freshly ground black pepper. Transfer the potatoes into the air fryer basket and air-fry for 30 minutes, turning the potatoes over halfway through the cooking process.
3. Remove the potatoes from the air fryer and let them rest for 5 minutes. Cut a large oval out of the top of both potatoes. Leaving half an inch of potato flesh around the edge of the potato, scoop the inside of the potato out and into a large bowl to prepare the potato filling. Mash the scooped potato filling with a fork and add the butter, sour cream, half-and-half, 1 cup of the grated Cheddar cheese, salt and pepper to taste. Mix well and then fold in the broccoli florets.
4. Stuff the hollowed out potato shells with the potato and broccoli mixture. Mound the filling high in the potatoes – you will have more filling than room in the potato shells.
5. Transfer the stuffed potatoes back to the air fryer basket and air-fry at 360°F for 10 minutes. Sprinkle the remaining Cheddar cheese on top of each stuffed potato, lower the heat to 330°F and air-fry for an additional minute or two to melt cheese.

# Cheese & Bean Burgers

Servings: 2
Cooking Time: 35 Minutes
**Ingredients:**

- 1 cup cooked black beans
- ½ cup shredded cheddar
- 1 egg, beaten
- Salt and pepper to taste
- 1 cup bread crumbs
- ½ cup grated carrots

**Directions:**

1. Preheat air fryer to 350°F. Mash the beans with a fork in a bowl. Mix in the cheese, salt, and pepper until evenly combined. Stir in half of the bread crumbs and egg. Shape the mixture into 2 patties. Coat each patty with the remaining bread crumbs and spray with cooking oil. Air Fry for 14-16 minutes, turning once. When ready, removeto a plate. Top with grated carrots and serve.

# Tomato & Squash Stuffed Mushrooms

Servings:2
Cooking Time: 15 Minutes
**Ingredients:**

- 12 whole white button mushrooms
- 3 tsp olive oil
- 2 tbsp diced zucchini
- 1 tsp soy sauce
- ¼ tsp salt
- 2 tbsp tomato paste
- 1 tbsp chopped parsley

**Directions:**

1. Preheat air fryer to 350ºF. Remove the stems from the mushrooms. Chop the stems finely and set in a bowl. Brush 1 tsp of olive oil around the top ridge of mushroom caps. To the bowl of the stem, add all ingredients, except for parsley, and mix. Divide and press mixture into tops of mushroom caps. Place the mushrooms in the frying basket and Air Fry for 5 minutes. Top with parsley. Serve.

# Tortilla Pizza Margherita

Servings: 1
Cooking Time: 15 Minutes
**Ingredients:**

- 1 flour tortilla
- ¼ cup tomato sauce
- 1/3 cup grated mozzarella
- 3 basil leaves

**Directions:**

1. Preheat air fryer to 350°F. Put the tortilla in the greased basket and pour the sauce in the center. Spread across the whole tortilla. Sprinkle with cheese and Bake for 8-10 minutes or until crisp. Remove carefully and top with basil leaves. Serve hot.

# Black Bean Stuffed Potato Boats

Servings: 4
Cooking Time: 55 Minutes
**Ingredients:**

- 4 russets potatoes
- 1 cup chipotle mayonnaise
- 1 cup canned black beans
- 2 tomatoes, chopped
- 1 scallion, chopped
- 1/3 cup chopped cilantro
- 1 poblano chile, minced
- 1 avocado, diced

**Directions:**

1. Preheat air fryer to 390°F. Clean the potatoes, poke with a fork, and spray with oil. Put in the air fryer and Bake for 30 minutes or until softened.
2. Heat the beans in a pan over medium heat. Put the potatoes on a plate and cut them across the top. Open them with a fork so you can stuff them. Top each potato with chipotle mayonnaise, beans, tomatoes, scallions, cilantro, poblano chile, and avocado. Serve immediately.

# Hearty Salad

Servings: 2
Cooking Time: 15 Minutes
**Ingredients:**
- 5 oz cauliflower, cut into florets
- 2 grated carrots
- 1 tbsp olive oil
- 1 tbsp lemon juice
- 2 tbsp raisins
- 2 tbsp roasted pepitas
- 2 tbsp diced red onion
- ¼ cup mayonnaise
- 1/8 tsp black pepper
- 1 tsp cumin
- ½ tsp chia seeds
- ½ tsp sesame seeds

**Directions:**
1. Preheat air fryer at 350ºF. Combine the cauliflower, cumin, olive oil, black pepper and lemon juice in a bowl, place it in the frying basket, and Bake for 5 minutes. Transfer it to a serving dish. Toss in the remaining ingredients. Let chill covered in the fridge until ready to use. Serve sprinkled with sesame and chia seeds.

# Honey Pear Chips

Servings: 4
Cooking Time: 30 Minutes
**Ingredients:**
- 2 firm pears, thinly sliced
- 1 tbsp lemon juice
- ½ tsp ground cinnamon
- 1 tsp honey

**Directions:**
1. Preheat air fryer to 380°F. Arrange the pear slices on the parchment-lined cooking basket. Drizzle with lemon juice and honey and sprinkle with cinnamon. Air Fry for 6-8 minutes, shaking the basket once, until golden. Leave to cool. Serve immediately or save for later in an airtight container. Good for 2 days.

# Veggie Samosas

Servings: 6
Cooking Time: 30 Minutes
**Ingredients:**
- 2 tbsp cream cheese, softened
- 3 tbsp minced onion
- 2 garlic cloves, minced
- 2 tbsp grated carrots
- 3 tsp olive oil
- 3 tbsp cooked green lentils
- 6 phyllo dough sheets

**Directions:**
1. Preheat air fryer to 390°F. Toss the onion, garlic, carrots, and some oil in a baking pan and stir. Place in the fryer and Air Fry for 2-4 minutes until the veggies are soft. Pour into a bowl. Add the lentils and cream cheese; let chill.
2. To make the dough, first lay a sheet of phyllo on a clean workspace and spritz with some olive oil, then add a second sheet on top. Repeat with the rest of the phyllo sheets until you have 3 stacks of 2 layers. Cut the stacks into 4 lengthwise strips. Add 2 tsp of the veggie mix at the bottom of each strip, then make a triangle by lifting one corner over the filling. Continue the triangle making, like folding a flag, and seal with water. Repeat until all strips are filled and folded. Bake the samosas in the air fryer for 4-7 minutes, until golden and crisp. Serve warm.

# Tacos

Servings: 24
Cooking Time: 8 Minutes Per Batch
**Ingredients:**
- 1 24-count package 4-inch corn tortillas
- 1½ cups refried beans (about ¾ of a 15-ounce can)
- 4 ounces sharp Cheddar cheese, grated
- ½ cup salsa
- oil for misting or cooking spray

**Directions:**
1. Preheat air fryer to 390°F.
2. Wrap refrigerated tortillas in damp paper towels and microwave for 30 to 60 seconds to warm. If necessary, rewarm tortillas as you go to keep them soft enough to fold without breaking.

3. Working with one tortilla at a time, top with 1 tablespoon of beans, 1 tablespoon of grated cheese, and 1 teaspoon of salsa. Fold over and press down very gently on the center. Press edges firmly all around to seal. Spray both sides with oil or cooking spray.

4. Cooking in two batches, place half the tacos in the air fryer basket. To cook 12 at a time, you may need to stand them upright and lean some against the sides of basket. It's okay if they're crowded as long as you leave a little room for air to circulate around them.

5. Cook for 8 minutes or until golden brown and crispy.

6. Repeat steps 4 and 5 to cook remaining tacos.

## Cheesy Veggie Frittata

Servings: 2
Cooking Time: 65 Minutes
**Ingredients:**

- 4 oz Bella mushrooms, chopped
- ¼ cup halved grape tomatoes
- 1 cup baby spinach
- 1/3 cup chopped leeks
- 1 baby carrot, chopped
- 4 eggs
- ½ cup grated cheddar
- 1 tbsp milk
- ¼ tsp garlic powder
- ¼ tsp dried oregano
- Salt and pepper to taste

**Directions:**

1. Preheat air fryer to 300°F. Crack the eggs into a bowl and beat them with a fork or whisk. Mix in the remaining ingredients until well combined. Pour into a greased cake pan. Put the pan into the frying basket and Bake for 20-23 minutes or until eggs are set in the center. Remove from the fryer. Cut into halves and serve.

## Healthy Living Mushroom Enchiladas

Servings: 4
Cooking Time: 40 Minutes
**Ingredients:**

- 2 cups sliced mushrooms
- ½ onion, thinly sliced
- 2 garlic cloves, minced
- 1 tbsp olive oil
- 10 oz spinach, chopped
- ½ tsp ground cumin
- 1 tbsp dried oregano
- 1 tsp chili powder
- ¼ cup grated feta cheese
- ¼ tsp red pepper flakes
- 1 cup grated mozzarella cheese
- 1 cup sour cream
- 2 tbsp mayonnaise
- Juice of 1 lime
- Salt and pepper to taste
- 8 corn tortillas
- 1 jalapeño pepper, diced
- ¼ cup chopped cilantro

**Directions:**

1. Preheat air fryer to 400°F. Combine mushrooms, onion, oregano, garlic, chili powder, olive oil, and salt in a small bowl until well coated. Transfer to the greased frying basket. Cook for 5 minutes, then shake the basket. Cook for another 3 to 4 minutes, then transfer to a medium bowl. Wipe out the frying basket. Take the garlic cloves from the mushroom mixture and finely mince them. Return half of the garlic to the bowl with the mushrooms. Stir in spinach, cumin, red pepper flakes, and ½ cup of mozzarella. Place the other half of the minced garlic in a small bowl along with sour cream, mayonnaise, feta, the rest of the mozzarella, lime juice, and black pepper.

2. To prepare the enchiladas, spoon 2 tablespoons of mushroom mixture in the center of each tortilla. Roll the tortilla and place it seam-side down in the baking dish. Repeat for the rest of the tortillas. Top with sour cream mixture and garnish with jalapenos. Place the dish in the frying basket and bake for 20 minutes until heated through and just brown on top. Top with cilantro. Serve.

# Vegan French Toast

Servings: 4
Cooking Time: 15 Minutes
Ingredients:

- 1 ripe banana, mashed
- ¼ cup protein powder
- ½ cup milk
- 2 tbsp ground flaxseed
- 4 bread slices
- 2 tbsp agave syrup

Directions:

1. Preheat air fryer to 370°F. Combine the banana, protein powder, milk, and flaxseed in a shallow bowl and mix well Dip bread slices into the mixture. Place the slices on a lightly greased pan in a single layer and pour any of the remaining mixture evenly over the bread. Air Fry for 10 minutes, or until golden brown and crispy, flipping once. Serve warm topped with agave syrup.

# Spaghetti Squash And Kale Fritters With Pomodoro Sauce

Servings: 3
Cooking Time: 45 Minutes
Ingredients:

- 1½-pound spaghetti squash (about half a large or a whole small squash)
- olive oil
- ½ onion, diced
- ½ red bell pepper, diced
- 2 cloves garlic, minced
- 4 cups coarsely chopped kale
- salt and freshly ground black pepper
- 1 egg
- ⅓ cup breadcrumbs, divided*
- ⅓ cup grated Parmesan cheese
- ½ teaspoon dried rubbed sage
- pinch nutmeg
- Pomodoro Sauce:
- 2 tablespoons olive oil
- ½ onion, chopped
- 1 to 2 cloves garlic, minced
- 1 (28-ounce) can peeled tomatoes
- ¼ cup red wine

- 1 teaspoon Italian seasoning
- 2 tablespoons chopped fresh basil, plus more for garnish
- salt and freshly ground black pepper
- ½ teaspoon sugar (optional)

Directions:

1. Preheat the air fryer to 370°F.
2. Cut the spaghetti squash in half lengthwise and remove the seeds. Rub the inside of the squash with olive oil and season with salt and pepper. Place the squash, cut side up, into the air fryer basket and air-fry for 30 minutes, flipping the squash over halfway through the cooking process.
3. While the squash is cooking, Preheat a large sauté pan over medium heat on the stovetop. Add a little olive oil and sauté the onions for 3 minutes, until they start to soften. Add the red pepper and garlic and continue to sauté for an additional 4 minutes. Add the kale and season with salt and pepper. Cook for 2 more minutes, or until the kale is soft. Transfer the mixture to a large bowl and let it cool.
4. While the squash continues to cook, make the Pomodoro sauce. Preheat the large sauté pan again over medium heat on the stovetop. Add the olive oil and sauté the onion and garlic for 2 to 3 minutes, until the onion begins to soften. Crush the canned tomatoes with your hands and add them to the pan along with the red wine and Italian seasoning and simmer for 20 minutes. Add the basil and season to taste with salt, pepper and sugar (if using).
5. When the spaghetti squash has finished cooking, use a fork to scrape the inside flesh of the squash onto a sheet pan. Spread the squash out and let it cool.
6. Once cool, add the spaghetti squash to the kale mixture, along with the egg, breadcrumbs, Parmesan cheese, sage, nutmeg, salt and freshly ground black pepper. Stir to combine well and then divide the mixture into 6 thick portions. You can shape the portions into patties, but I prefer to keep them a little random and unique in shape. Spray or brush the fritters with olive oil.
7. Preheat the air fryer to 370°F.
8. Brush the air fryer basket with a little olive oil and transfer the fritters to the basket. Air-fry the squash and kale fritters at 370°F for 15 minutes, flipping them over halfway through the cooking process.
9. Serve the fritters warm with the Pomodoro sauce spooned over the top or pooled on your plate. Garnish with the fresh basil leaves.

# Basil Green Beans

Servings: 4
Cooking Time: 15 Minutes
**Ingredients:**

- 1 ½ lb green beans, trimmed
- 1 tbsp olive oil
- 1 tbsp fresh basil, chopped
- Garlic salt to taste

**Directions:**

1. Preheat air fryer to 400°F. Coat the green beans with olive oil in a large bowl. Combine with fresh basil powder and garlic salt. Put the beans in the frying basket and Air Fry for 7-9 minutes, shaking once until the beans begin to brown. Serve warm and enjoy!

# Spicy Bean Patties

Servings: 4
Cooking Time: 20 Minutes

**Ingredients:**

- 1 cup canned black beans
- 1 bread slice, torn
- 2 tbsp spicy brown mustard
- 1 tbsp chili powder
- 1 egg white
- 2 tbsp grated carrots
- ¼ diced green bell pepper
- 1-2 jalapeño peppers, diced
- ¼ tsp ground cumin
- ¼ tsp smoked paprika
- 2 tbsp cream cheese
- 1 tbsp olive oil

**Directions:**

1. Preheat air fryer at 350ºF. Using a fork, mash beans until smooth. Stir in the remaining ingredients, except olive oil. Form mixture into 4 patties. Place bean patties in the greased frying basket and Air Fry for 6 minutes, turning once, and brush with olive oil. Serve immediately.

# Desserts And Sweets Recipes

## Date Oat Cookies

Servings: 6
Cooking Time: 20 Minutes
**Ingredients:**
- ¼ cup butter, softened
- 2 ½ tbsp milk
- ½ cup sugar
- ½ tsp vanilla extract
- ½ tsp lemon zest
- ½ tsp ground cinnamon
- 3/4 cup flour
- ¼ tsp salt
- ¾ cup rolled oats
- ¼ tsp baking soda
- ¼ tsp baking powder
- 2 tbsp dates, chopped

**Directions:**

1. Use an electric beater to whip the butter until fluffy. Add the milk, sugar, lemon zest, and vanilla. Stir until well combined. Add the cinnamon, flour, salt, oats, baking soda, and baking powder in a separate bowl and stir. Add the dry mix to the wet mix and stir with a wooden spoon. Pour in the dates.

2. Preheat air fryer to 350°F. Drop tablespoonfuls of the batter onto a greased baking pan, leaving room in between each. Bake for 6 minutes or until light brown. Make all the cookies at once, or save the batter in the fridge for later. Let them cool and enjoy!

## Chocolate Soufflés

Servings: 2
Cooking Time: 14 Minutes
**Ingredients:**
- butter and sugar for greasing the ramekins
- 3 ounces semi-sweet chocolate, chopped
- ¼ cup unsalted butter
- 2 eggs, yolks and white separated
- 3 tablespoons sugar
- ½ teaspoon pure vanilla extract
- 2 tablespoons all-purpose flour
- powdered sugar, for dusting the finished soufflés
- heavy cream, for serving

**Directions:**

1. Butter and sugar two 6-ounce ramekins. (Butter the ramekins and then coat the butter with sugar by shaking it around in the ramekin and dumping out any excess.)

2. Melt the chocolate and butter together, either in the microwave or in a double boiler. In a separate bowl, beat the egg yolks vigorously. Add the sugar and the vanilla extract and beat well again. Drizzle in the chocolate and butter, mixing well. Stir in the flour, combining until there are no lumps.

3. Preheat the air fryer to 330°F.

4. In a separate bowl, whisk the egg whites to soft peak stage (the point at which the whites can almost stand up on the end of your whisk). Fold the whipped egg whites into the chocolate mixture gently and in stages.

5. Transfer the batter carefully to the buttered ramekins, leaving about ½-inch at the top. (You may have a little extra batter, depending on how airy the batter is, so you might be able to squeeze out a third soufflé if you want to.) Place the ramekins into the air fryer basket and air-fry for 14 minutes. The soufflés should have risen nicely and be brown on top. (Don't worry if the top gets a little dark – you'll be covering it with powdered sugar in the next step.)

6. Dust with powdered sugar and serve immediately with heavy cream to pour over the top at the table.

## Vanilla Butter Cake

Servings: 6
Cooking Time: 20-24 Minutes
**Ingredients:**
- ¾ cup plus 1 tablespoon All-purpose flour
- 1 teaspoon Baking powder
- ¼ teaspoon Table salt
- 8 tablespoons (½ cup/1 stick) Butter, at room temperature
- ½ cup Granulated white sugar
- 2 Large egg(s)
- 2 tablespoons Whole or low-fat milk (not fat-free)
- ¾ teaspoon Vanilla extract
- Baking spray (see here)

**Directions:**

1. Preheat the air fryer to 325°F (or 330°F, if that's the closest setting).

2. Mix the flour, baking powder, and salt in a small bowl until well combined.

3. Using an electric hand mixer at medium speed, beat the butter and sugar in a medium bowl until creamy and smooth, about 3 minutes, occasionally scraping down the inside of the bowl.

4. Beat in the egg or eggs, as well as the white or a yolk as necessary. Beat in the milk and vanilla until smooth. Turn off the beaters and add the flour mixture. Beat at low speed until thick and smooth.

5. Use the baking spray to generously coat the inside of a 6-inch round cake pan for a small batch, a 7-inch round cake pan for a medium batch, or an 8-inch round cake pan for a large batch. Scrape and spread the batter into the pan, smoothing the batter out to an even layer.

6. Set the pan in the basket and air-fry undisturbed for 20 minutes for a 6-inch layer, 22 minutes for a 7-inch layer, or 24 minutes for an 8-inch layer, or until a toothpick or cake tester inserted into the center of the cake comes out clean. Start checking it at the 15-minute mark to know where you are.

7. Use hot pads or silicone baking mitts to transfer the cake pan to a wire rack. Cool for 5 minutes. To unmold, set a cutting board over the baking pan and invert both the board and the pan. Lift the still-warm pan off the cake layer. Set the wire rack on top of the cake layer and invert all of it with the cutting board so that the cake layer is now right side up on the wire rack. Remove the cutting board and continue cooling the cake for at least 10 minutes or to room temperature, about 30 minutes, before slicing into wedges.

- 2½ tablespoons Tahini (see here)
- 2½ tablespoons Maple syrup
- 2 teaspoons Vanilla extract
- ⅔ cup Vegan semisweet or bittersweet chocolate chips
- Baking spray

**Directions:**

1. Preheat the air fryer to 325°F (or 330°F, if that's the closest setting).

2. Whisk the flour, oats, baking soda, and salt in a bowl until well combined.

3. Using an electric hand mixer at medium speed, beat the sugar, oil, tahini, maple syrup, and vanilla until rich and creamy, about 3 minutes, scraping down the inside of the bowl occasionally.

4. Scrape down and remove the beaters. Fold in the flour mixture and chocolate chips with a rubber spatula just until all the flour is moistened and the chocolate chips are even throughout the dough.

5. For a small air fryer, coat the inside of a 6-inch round cake pan with baking spray. For a medium air fryer, coat the inside of a 7-inch round cake pan with baking spray. And for a large air fryer, coat the inside of an 8-inch round cake pan with baking spray. Scrape and gently press the dough into the prepared pan, spreading it into an even layer to the perimeter.

6. Set the pan in the basket and air-fry undisturbed for 16 minutes, or until puffed, browned, and firm to the touch.

7. Transfer the pan to a wire rack and cool for 10 minutes. Loosen the cookie from the perimeter with a spatula, then invert the pan onto a cutting board and let the cookie come free. Remove the pan and reinvert the cookie onto the wire rack. Cool for 5 minutes more before slicing into wedges to serve.

## Giant Vegan Chocolate Chip Cookie

Servings: 4
Cooking Time: 16 Minutes
**Ingredients:**

- ⅔ cup All-purpose flour
- 5 tablespoons Rolled oats (not quick-cooking or steel-cut oats)
- ¼ teaspoon Baking soda
- ¼ teaspoon Table salt
- 5 tablespoons Granulated white sugar
- ¼ cup Vegetable oil

## Blueberry Cheesecake Tartlets

Servings: 9
Cooking Time: 6 Minutes
**Ingredients:**

- 8 ounces cream cheese, softened
- ¼ cup sugar
- 1 egg
- ½ teaspoon vanilla extract
- zest of 2 lemons, divided
- 9 mini graham cracker tartlet shells*

- 2 cups blueberries
- ½ teaspoon ground cinnamon
- juice of ½ lemon
- ¼ cup apricot preserves

**Directions:**

1. Preheat the air fryer to 330°F.
2. Combine the cream cheese, sugar, egg, vanilla and the zest of one lemon in a medium bowl and blend until smooth by hand or with an electric hand mixer. Pour the cream cheese mixture into the tartlet shells.
3. Air-fry 3 tartlets at a time at 330°F for 6 minutes, rotating them in the air fryer basket halfway through the cooking time.
4. Combine the blueberries, cinnamon, zest of one lemon and juice of half a lemon in a bowl. Melt the apricot preserves in the microwave or over low heat in a saucepan. Pour the apricot preserves over the blueberries and gently toss to coat.
5. Allow the cheesecakes to cool completely and then top each one with some of the blueberry mixture. Garnish the tartlets with a little sugared lemon peel and refrigerate until you are ready to serve.

# Apple & Blueberry Crumble

Servings: 4
Cooking Time: 20 Minutes
**Ingredients:**

- 5 apples, peeled and diced
- ½ lemon, zested and juiced
- ½ cup blueberries
- 1 cup brown sugar
- 1 tsp cinnamon
- ½ cup butter
- ½ cup flour

**Directions:**

1. Preheat air fryer to 340°F. Place the apple chunks, blueberries, lemon juice and zest, half of the butter, half of the brown sugar, and cinnamon in a greased baking dish. Combine thoroughly until all is well mixed. Combine the flour with the remaining butter and brown sugar in a separate bowl. Stir until it forms a crumbly consistency. Spread the mixture over the fruit. Bake in the air fryer for 10-15 minutes until golden and bubbling. Serve and enjoy!

# Nutty Banana Bread

Servings: 6
Cooking Time: 30 Minutes
**Ingredients:**

- 2 bananas
- 2 tbsp ground flaxseed
- ¼ cup milk
- 1 tbsp apple cider vinegar
- 1 tbsp vanilla extract
- ½ tsp ground cinnamon
- 2 tbsp honey
- ½ cup oat flour
- ½ tsp baking soda
- 3 tbsp butter

**Directions:**

1. Preheat air fryer to 320°F. Using a fork, mash the bananas until chunky. Mix in flaxseed, milk, apple vinegar, vanilla extract, cinnamon, and honey. Finally, toss in oat flour and baking soda until smooth but still chunky. Divide the batter between 6 cupcake molds. Top with one and a half teaspoons of butter each and swirl it a little. Bake for 18 minutes until golden brown and puffy. Let cool completely before serving.

# Custard

Servings: 4
Cooking Time: 45 Minutes
**Ingredients:**

- 2 cups whole milk
- 2 eggs
- ¼ cup sugar
- ⅛ teaspoon salt
- ¼ teaspoon vanilla
- cooking spray
- ⅛ teaspoon nutmeg

**Directions:**

1. In a blender, process milk, egg, sugar, salt, and vanilla until smooth.

2. Spray a 6 x 6-inch baking pan with nonstick spray and pour the custard into it.

3. Cook at 300°F for 45 minutes. Custard is done when the center sets.

4. Sprinkle top with the nutmeg.

5. Allow custard to cool slightly.

6. Serve it warm, at room temperature, or chilled.

# One-bowl Chocolate Buttermilk Cake

Servings: 6

Cooking Time: 16-20 Minutes

**Ingredients:**

- ¾ cup All-purpose flour
- ½ cup Granulated white sugar
- 3 tablespoons Unsweetened cocoa powder
- ½ teaspoon Baking soda
- ¼ teaspoon Table salt
- ½ cup Buttermilk
- 2 tablespoons Vegetable oil
- ¾ teaspoon Vanilla extract
- Baking spray (see here)

**Directions:**

1. Preheat the air fryer to 325°F (or 330°F, if that's the closest setting).

2. Stir the flour, sugar, cocoa powder, baking soda, and salt in a large bowl until well combined. Add the buttermilk, oil, and vanilla. Stir just until a thick, grainy batter forms.

3. Use the baking spray to generously coat the inside of a 6-inch round cake pan for a small batch, a 7-inch round cake pan for a medium batch, or an 8-inch round cake pan for a large batch. Scrape and spread the chocolate batter into this pan, smoothing the batter out to an even layer.

4. Set the pan in the basket and air-fry undisturbed for 16 minutes for a 6-inch layer, 18 minutes for a 7-inch layer, or 20 minutes for an 8-inch layer, or until a toothpick or cake tester inserted into the center of the cake comes out clean. Start checking it at the 14-minute mark to know where you are.

5. Use hot pads or silicone baking mitts to transfer the cake pan to a wire rack. Cool for 5 minutes. To unmold, set a cutting board over the baking pan and invert both the board and the pan. Lift the still-warm pan off the cake layer. Set the wire rack on top of the cake layer and invert all of it with the cutting board so that the cake layer is now right side up on the wire rack. Remove the cutting board and continue cooling the cake for at least 10 minutes or to room temperature, about 30 minutes, before slicing into wedges.

# Gingerbread

Servings: 6

Cooking Time: 20 Minutes

**Ingredients:**

- cooking spray
- 1 cup flour
- 2 tablespoons sugar
- ¾ teaspoon ground ginger
- ¼ teaspoon cinnamon
- 1 teaspoon baking powder
- ½ teaspoon baking soda
- ⅛ teaspoon salt
- 1 egg
- ¼ cup molasses
- ½ cup buttermilk
- 2 tablespoons oil
- 1 teaspoon pure vanilla extract

**Directions:**

1. Preheat air fryer to 330°F.

2. Spray 6 x 6-inch baking dish lightly with cooking spray.

3. In a medium bowl, mix together all the dry ingredients.

4. In a separate bowl, beat the egg. Add molasses, buttermilk, oil, and vanilla and stir until well mixed.

5. Pour liquid mixture into dry ingredients and stir until well blended.

6. Pour batter into baking dish and cook at 330°F for 20minutes or until toothpick inserted in center of loaf comes out clean.

# Peach Cobbler

Servings: 4
Cooking Time: 12 Minutes
**Ingredients:**
- 16 ounces frozen peaches, thawed, with juice (do not drain)
- 6 tablespoons sugar
- 1 tablespoon cornstarch
- 1 tablespoon water
- Crust
- ½ cup flour
- ¼ teaspoon salt
- 3 tablespoons butter
- 1½ tablespoons cold water
- ¼ teaspoon sugar

**Directions:**
1. Place peaches, including juice, and sugar in air fryer baking pan. Stir to mix well.
2. In a small cup, dissolve cornstarch in the water. Stir into peaches.
3. In a medium bowl, combine the flour and salt. Cut in butter using knives or a pastry blender. Stir in the cold water to make a stiff dough.
4. On a floured board or wax paper, pat dough into a square or circle slightly smaller than your air fryer baking pan. Cut diagonally into 4 pieces.
5. Place dough pieces on top of peaches, leaving a tiny bit of space between the edges. Sprinkle very lightly with sugar, no more than about ¼ teaspoon.
6. Cook at 360°F for 12 minutes, until fruit bubbles and crust browns.

# Party S´mores

Servings: 6
Cooking Time: 15 Minutes
**Ingredients:**
- 2 dark chocolate bars, cut into 12 pieces
- 12 buttermilk biscuits
- 12 marshmallows

**Directions:**
1. Preheat air fryer to 350°F. Place 6 biscuits in the air fryer. Top each square with a piece of dark chocolate. Bake for 2 minutes. Add a marshmallow to each piece of chocolate. Cook for another minute. Remove and top with another piece of biscuit. Serve warm.

# Coconut Macaroons

Servings: 12
Cooking Time: 8 Minutes
**Ingredients:**
- 1⅓ cups shredded, sweetened coconut
- 4½ teaspoons flour
- 2 tablespoons sugar
- 1 egg white
- ½ teaspoon almond extract

**Directions:**
1. Preheat air fryer to 330°F.
2. Mix all ingredients together.
3. Shape coconut mixture into 12 balls.
4. Place all 12 macaroons in air fryer basket. They won't expand, so you can place them close together, but they shouldn't touch.
5. Cook at 330°F for 8 minutes, until golden.

# Fruit Turnovers

Servings: 6
Cooking Time: 25 Minutes
**Ingredients:**
- 1 sheet puff pastry dough
- 6 tsp peach preserves
- 3 kiwi, sliced
- 1 large egg, beaten
- 1 tbsp icing sugar

**Directions:**
1. Prepare puff pastry by cutting it into 6 rectangles. Roll out the pastry with a rolling pin into 5-inch squares. On your workspace, position one square so that it looks like a diamond with points to the top and bottom. Spoon 1 tsp of the preserves on the bottom half and spread it, leaving a ½-inch border from the edge. Place half of one kiwi on top of the preserves. Brush the clean edges with the egg, then fold the top corner over the filling to make a triangle. Crimp with

87

a fork to seal the pastry. Brush the top of the pastry with egg. Preheat air fryer to 350°F. Put the pastries in the greased frying basket. Air Fry for 10 minutes, flipping once until golden and puffy. Remove from the fryer, let cool and dush with icing sugar. Serve.

# Fried Pineapple Chunks

Servings: 3
Cooking Time: 10 Minutes
**Ingredients:**
- 3 tablespoons Cornstarch
- 1 Large egg white, beaten until foamy
- 1 cup (4 ounces) Ground vanilla wafer cookies (not low-fat cookies)
- ¼ teaspoon Ground dried ginger
- 18 (about 2¼ cups) Fresh 1-inch chunks peeled and cored pineapple

**Directions:**
1. Preheat the air fryer to 400°F.
2. Put the cornstarch in a medium or large bowl. Put the beaten egg white in a small bowl. Pour the cookie crumbs and ground dried ginger into a large zip-closed plastic bag, shaking it a bit to combine them.
3. Dump the pineapple chunks into the bowl with the cornstarch. Toss and stir until well coated. Use your cleaned fingers or a large fork like a shovel to pick up a few pineapple chunks, shake off any excess cornstarch, and put them in the bowl with the egg white. Stir gently, then pick them up and let any excess egg white slip back into the rest. Put them in the bag with the crumb mixture. Repeat the cornstarch-then-egg process until all the pineapple chunks are in the bag. Seal the bag and shake gently, turning the bag this way and that, to coat the pieces well.
4. Set the coated pineapple chunks in the basket with as much air space between them as possible. Even a fraction of an inch will work, but they should not touch. Air-fry undisturbed for 10 minutes, or until golden brown and crisp.
5. Gently dump the contents of the basket onto a wire rack. Cool for at least 5 minutes or up to 15 minutes before serving.

# Nutella® Torte

Servings: 6
Cooking Time: 55 Minutes
**Ingredients:**
- ¼ cup unsalted butter, softened
- ½ cup sugar
- 2 eggs
- 1 teaspoon vanilla
- 1¼ cups Nutella® (or other chocolate hazelnut spread), divided
- ¼ cup flour
- 1 teaspoon baking powder
- ¼ teaspoon salt
- dark chocolate fudge topping
- coarsely chopped toasted hazelnuts

**Directions:**
1. Cream the butter and sugar together with an electric hand mixer until light and fluffy. Add the eggs, vanilla, and ¾ cup of the Nutella® and mix until combined. Combine the flour, baking powder and salt together, and add these dry ingredients to the butter mixture, beating for 1 minute.
2. Preheat the air fryer to 350°F.
3. Grease a 7-inch cake pan with butter and then line the bottom of the pan with a circle of parchment paper. Grease the parchment paper circle as well. Pour the batter into the prepared cake pan and wrap the pan completely with aluminum foil. Lower the pan into the air fryer basket with an aluminum sling (fold a piece of aluminum foil into a strip about 2-inches wide by 24-inches long). Fold the ends of the aluminum foil over the top of the dish before returning the basket to the air fryer. Air-fry for 30 minutes. Remove the foil and air-fry for another 25 minutes.
4. Remove the cake from air fryer and let it cool for 10 minutes. Invert the cake onto a plate, remove the parchment paper and invert the cake back onto a serving platter. While the cake is still warm, spread the remaining ½ cup of Nutella® over the top of the cake. Melt the dark chocolate fudge in the microwave for about 10 seconds so it melts enough to be pourable. Drizzle the sauce on top of the cake in a zigzag motion. Turn the cake 90 degrees and drizzle more sauce in zigzags perpendicular to the first zigzags. Garnish the edges of the torte with the toasted hazelnuts and serve.

# Annie's Chocolate Chunk Hazelnut Cookies

Servings: 24
Cooking Time: 12 Minutes
**Ingredients:**

- 1 cup butter, softened
- 1 cup brown sugar
- ½ cup granulated sugar
- 2 eggs, lightly beaten
- 1½ teaspoons vanilla extract
- 1½ cups all-purpose flour
- ½ cup rolled oats
- 1 teaspoon baking soda
- ½ teaspoon salt
- 2 cups chocolate chunks
- ½ cup toasted chopped hazelnuts

**Directions:**

1. Cream the butter and sugars together until light and fluffy using a stand mixer or electric hand mixer. Add the eggs and vanilla, and beat until well combined.
2. Combine the flour, rolled oats, baking soda and salt in a second bowl. Gradually add the dry ingredients to the wet ingredients with a wooden spoon or spatula. Stir in the chocolate chunks and hazelnuts until distributed throughout the dough.
3. Shape the cookies into small balls about the size of golf balls and place them on a baking sheet. Freeze the cookie balls for at least 30 minutes, or package them in as airtight a package as you can and keep them in your freezer.
4. When you're ready for a delicious snack or dessert, Preheat the air fryer to 350°F. Cut a piece of parchment paper to fit the number of cookies you are baking. Place the parchment down in the air fryer basket and place the frozen cookie ball or balls on top (remember to leave room for them to expand).
5. Air-fry the cookies at 350°F for 12 minutes, or until they are done to your liking. Let them cool for a few minutes before enjoying your freshly baked cookie.

# Fried Cannoli Wontons

Servings: 10
Cooking Time: 8 Minutes
**Ingredients:**

- 8 ounces Neufchâtel cream cheese
- ¼ cup powdered sugar
- 1 teaspoon vanilla extract
- ¼ teaspoon salt
- ¼ cup mini chocolate chips
- 2 tablespoons chopped pecans (optional)
- 20 wonton wrappers
- ¼ cup filtered water

**Directions:**

1. Preheat the air fryer to 370°F.
2. In a large bowl, use a hand mixer to combine the cream cheese with the powdered sugar, vanilla, and salt. Fold in the chocolate chips and pecans. Set aside.
3. Lay the wonton wrappers out on a flat, smooth surface and place a bowl with the filtered water next to them.
4. Use a teaspoon to evenly divide the cream cheese mixture among the 20 wonton wrappers, placing the batter in the center of the wontons.
5. Wet the tip of your index finger, and gently moisten the outer edges of the wrapper. Then fold each wrapper until it creates a secure pocket.
6. Liberally spray the air fryer basket with olive oil mist.
7. Place the wontons into the basket, and cook for 5 to 8 minutes. When the outer edges begin to brown, remove the wontons from the air fryer basket. Repeat cooking with remaining wontons.
8. Serve warm.

# Cheesecake Wontons

Servings:16
Cooking Time: 6 Minutes
**Ingredients:**

- ¼ cup Regular or low-fat cream cheese (not fat-free)
- 2 tablespoons Granulated white sugar
- 1½ tablespoons Egg yolk
- ¼ teaspoon Vanilla extract
- ⅛ teaspoon Table salt
- 1½ tablespoons All-purpose flour
- 16 Wonton wrappers (vegetarian, if a concern)
- Vegetable oil spray

**Directions:**

1. Preheat the air fryer to 400°F.

2. Using a flatware fork, mash the cream cheese, sugar, egg yolk, and vanilla in a small bowl until smooth. Add the salt and flour and continue mashing until evenly combined.

3. Set a wonton wrapper on a clean, dry work surface so that one corner faces you (so that it looks like a diamond on your work surface). Set 1 teaspoon of the cream cheese mixture in the middle of the wrapper but just above a horizontal line that would divide the wrapper in half. Dip your clean finger in water and run it along the edges of the wrapper. Fold the corner closest to you up and over the filling, lining it up with the corner farthest from you, thereby making a stuffed triangle. Press gently to seal. Wet the two triangle tips nearest you, then fold them up and together over the filling. Gently press together to seal and fuse. Set aside and continue making more stuffed wontons, 11 more for the small batch, 15 more for the medium batch, or 23 more for the large one.

4. Lightly coat the stuffed wrappers on all sides with vegetable oil spray. Set them with the fused corners up in the basket with as much air space between them as possible. Air-fry undisturbed for 6 minutes, or until golden brown and crisp.

5. Gently dump the contents of the basket onto a wire rack. Cool for at least 5 minutes before serving.

## Baked Caramelized Peaches

Servings: 6
Cooking Time: 25 Minutes
**Ingredients:**

- 3 pitted peaches, halved
- 2 tbsp brown sugar
- 1 cup heavy cream
- 1 tsp vanilla extract
- ¼ tsp ground cinnamon
- 1 cup fresh blueberries

**Directions:**

1. Preheat air fryer to 380°F. Lay the peaches in the frying basket with the cut side up, then top them with brown sugar. Bake for 7-11 minutes, allowing the peaches to brown around the edges. In a mixing bowl, whisk heavy cream, vanilla, and cinnamon until stiff peaks form. Fold the peaches into a plate. Spoon the cream mixture into the peach cups, top with blueberries, and serve.

## Maple Cinnamon Cheesecake

Servings: 4
Cooking Time: 12 Minutes
**Ingredients:**

- 6 sheets of cinnamon graham crackers
- 2 tablespoons butter
- 8 ounces Neufchâtel cream cheese
- 3 tablespoons pure maple syrup
- 1 large egg
- ½ teaspoon ground cinnamon
- ¼ teaspoon salt

**Directions:**

1. Preheat the air fryer to 350°F.

2. Place the graham crackers in a food processor and process until crushed into a flour. Mix with the butter and press into a mini air-fryer-safe pan lined at the bottom with parchment paper. Place in the air fryer and cook for 4 minutes.

3. In a large bowl, place the cream cheese and maple syrup. Use a hand mixer or stand mixer and beat together until smooth. Add in the egg, cinnamon, and salt and mix on medium speed until combined.

4. Remove the graham cracker crust from the air fryer and pour the batter into the pan.

5. Place the pan back in the air fryer, adjusting the temperature to 315°F. Cook for 18 minutes. Carefully remove when cooking completes. The top should be lightly browned and firm.

6. Keep the cheesecake in the pan and place in the refrigerator for 3 or more hours to firm up before serving.

## Lemon Iced Donut Balls

Servings: 6
Cooking Time: 25 Minutes
**Ingredients:**

- 1 can jumbo biscuit dough
- 2 tsp lemon juice
- ½ cup icing sugar, sifted

**Directions:**

1. Preheat air fryer to 360°F. Divide the biscuit dough into 16 equal portions. Roll the dough into balls of 1½ inches

thickness. Place the donut holes in the greased frying basket and Air Fry for 8 minutes, flipping once. Mix the icing sugar and lemon juice until smooth. Spread the icing over the top of the donuts. Leave to set a bit. Serve.

# Struffoli

Servings: X
Cooking Time: 20 Minutes

**Ingredients:**

- ¼ cup butter, softened
- ⅔ cup sugar
- 5 eggs
- 2 teaspoons vanilla extract
- zest of 1 lemon
- 4 cups all-purpose flour
- 2 teaspoons baking soda
- ¼ teaspoon salt
- 16 ounces honey
- 1 teaspoon ground cinnamon
- zest of 1 orange
- 2 tablespoons water
- nonpareils candy sprinkles

**Directions:**

1. Cream the butter and sugar together in a bowl until light and fluffy using a hand mixer (or a stand mixer). Add the eggs, vanilla and lemon zest and mix. In a separate bowl, combine the flour, baking soda and salt. Add the dry ingredients to the wet ingredients and mix until you have a soft dough. Shape the dough into a ball, wrap it in plastic and let it rest for 30 minutes.

2. Divide the dough ball into four pieces. Roll each piece into a long rope. Cut each rope into about 25 (½-inch) pieces. Roll each piece into a tight ball. You should have 100 little balls when finished.

3. Preheat the air fryer to 370°F.

4. In batches of about 20, transfer the dough balls to the air fryer basket, leaving a small space in between them. Air-fry the dough balls at 370°F for 3 to 4 minutes, shaking the basket when one minute of cooking time remains.

5. After all the dough balls are air-fried, make the honey topping. Melt the honey in a small saucepan on the stovetop. Add the cinnamon, orange zest, and water. Simmer for one minute. Place the air-fried dough balls in a large bowl and drizzle the honey mixture over top. Gently toss to coat all

the dough balls evenly. Transfer the coated struffoli to a platter and sprinkle the nonpareil candy sprinkles over top. You can dress the presentation up by piling the balls into the shape of a wreath or pile them high in a cone shape to resemble a Christmas tree.

6. Struffoli can be made ahead. Store covered tightly.

# Baked Apple

Servings: 6
Cooking Time: 20 Minutes

**Ingredients:**

- 3 small Honey Crisp or other baking apples
- 3 tablespoons maple syrup
- 3 tablespoons chopped pecans
- 1 tablespoon firm butter, cut into 6 pieces

**Directions:**

1. Put ½ cup water in the drawer of the air fryer.
2. Wash apples well and dry them.
3. Split apples in half. Remove core and a little of the flesh to make a cavity for the pecans.
4. Place apple halves in air fryer basket, cut side up.
5. Spoon 1½ teaspoons pecans into each cavity.
6. Spoon ½ tablespoon maple syrup over pecans in each apple.
7. Top each apple with ½ teaspoon butter.
8. Cook at 360°F for 20 minutes, until apples are tender.

# Caramel Apple Crumble

Servings: 6
Cooking Time: 50 Minutes

**Ingredients:**

- 4 apples, peeled and thinly sliced
- 2 tablespoons sugar
- 1 tablespoon flour
- 1 teaspoon ground cinnamon
- ¼ teaspoon ground allspice
- healthy pinch ground nutmeg
- 10 caramel squares, cut into small pieces
- Crumble Topping:
- ¾ cup rolled oats
- ¼ cup sugar

- ⅓ cup flour
- ¼ teaspoon ground cinnamon
- 6 tablespoons butter, melted

**Directions:**

1. Preheat the air fryer to 330°F.
2. Combine the apples, sugar, flour, and spices in a large bowl and toss to coat. Add the caramel pieces and mix well. Pour the apple mixture into a 1-quart round baking dish that will fit in your air fryer basket (6-inch diameter).
3. To make the crumble topping, combine the rolled oats, sugar, flour and cinnamon in a small bowl. Add the melted butter and mix well. Top the apples with the crumble mixture. Cover the entire dish with aluminum foil and transfer the dish to the air fryer basket, lowering the dish into the basket using a sling made of aluminum foil (fold a piece of aluminum foil into a strip about 2-inches wide by 24-inches long). Fold the ends of the aluminum foil over the top of the dish before returning the basket to the air fryer.
4. Air-fry at 330°F for 25 minutes. Remove the aluminum foil and continue to air-fry for another 25 minutes. Serve the crumble warm with whipped cream or vanilla ice cream, if desired.

# Banana Fritters

Servings: 6
Cooking Time: 20 Minutes
**Ingredients:**

- 1 egg
- ¼ cup cornstarch
- ¼ cup bread crumbs
- 3 bananas, halved crosswise
- ¼ cup caramel sauce

**Directions:**

1. Preheat air fryer to 350°F. Set up three small bowls. In the first bowl, add cornstarch. In the second bowl, beat the egg. In the third bowl, add bread crumbs. Dip the bananas in the cornstarch first, then the egg, and then dredge in bread crumbs. Put the bananas in the greased frying basket and spray with oil. Air Fry for 8 minutes, flipping once around minute 5. Remove to a serving plate and drizzle with caramel sauce. Serve warm and enjoy.

# Cinnamon Canned Biscuit Donuts

Servings: 4
Cooking Time: 25 Minutes
**Ingredients:**

- 1 can jumbo biscuits
- 1 cup cinnamon sugar

**Directions:**

1. Preheat air fryer to 360°F. Divide biscuit dough into 8 biscuits and place on a flat work surface. Cut a small circle in the center of the biscuit with a small cookie cutter. Place a batch of 4 donuts in the air fryer. Spray with oil and Bake for 8 minutes, flipping once. Drizzle the cinnamon sugar over the donuts and serve.

# Vegan Brownie Bites

Servings: 10
Cooking Time: 8 Minutes
**Ingredients:**

- ⅔ cup walnuts
- ⅓ cup all-purpose flour
- ¼ cup dark cocoa powder
- ⅓ cup cane sugar
- ¼ teaspoon salt
- 2 tablespoons vegetable oil
- 1 teaspoon pure vanilla extract
- 1 tablespoon almond milk
- 1 tablespoon powdered sugar

**Directions:**

1. Preheat the air fryer to 350°F.
2. To a blender or food processor fitted with a metal blade, add the walnuts, flour, cocoa powder, sugar, and salt. Pulse until smooth, about 30 seconds. Add in the oil, vanilla, and milk and pulse until a dough is formed.
3. Remove the dough and place in a bowl. Form into 10 equal-size bites.
4. Liberally spray the metal trivet in the air fryer basket with olive oil mist. Place the brownie bites into the basket and cook for 8 minutes, or until the outer edges begin to slightly crack.
5. Remove the basket from the air fryer and let cool. Sprinkle the brownie bites with powdered sugar and serve.

# Honeyed Tortilla Fritters

Servings: 8
Cooking Time: 10 Minutes
**Ingredients:**

- 2 tbsp granulated sugar
- ½ tsp ground cinnamon
- 1 tsp vanilla powder
- Salt to taste
- 8 flour tortillas, quartered
- 2 tbsp butter, melted
- 4 tsp honey
- 1 tbsp almond flakes

**Directions:**

1. Preheat air fryer at 400°F. Combine the sugar, cinnamon, vanilla powder, and salt in a bowl. Set aside. Brush tortilla quarters with melted butter and sprinkle with sugar mixture. Place tortilla quarters in the frying basket and Air Fry for 4 minutes, turning once. Let cool on a large plate for 5 minutes until hardened. Drizzle with honey and scatter with almond flakes to serve.

# Honey-roasted Mixed Nuts

Servings: 8
Cooking Time: 15 Minutes
**Ingredients:**

- ½ cup raw, shelled pistachios
- ½ cup raw almonds
- 1 cup raw walnuts
- 2 tablespoons filtered water
- 2 tablespoons honey
- 1 tablespoon vegetable oil
- 2 tablespoons sugar
- ½ teaspoon salt

**Directions:**

1. Preheat the air fryer to 300°F.
2. Lightly spray an air-fryer-safe pan with olive oil; then place the pistachios, almonds, and walnuts inside the pan and place the pan inside the air fryer basket.
3. Cook for 15 minutes, shaking the basket every 5 minutes to rotate the nuts.
4. While the nuts are roasting, boil the water in a small pan and stir in the honey and oil. Continue to stir while cooking until the water begins to evaporate and a thick sauce is formed. Note: The sauce should stick to the back of a wooden spoon when mixed. Turn off the heat.
5. Remove the nuts from the air fryer (cooking should have just completed) and spoon the nuts into the stovetop pan. Use a spatula to coat the nuts with the honey syrup.
6. Line a baking sheet with parchment paper and spoon the nuts onto the sheet. Lightly sprinkle the sugar and salt over the nuts and let cool in the refrigerator for at least 2 hours.
7. When the honey and sugar have hardened, store the nuts in an airtight container in the refrigerator.

# RECIPES INDEX

# D

# E

# F

# G

# S

# T

# V

# W

# Y

# Z

Printed in Great Britain
by Amazon

37255359R00057

# SCHOLAST

# READ & RESI

## Bringing the best books to life in the classroom

**Activities based on**

**The Jungle Book**

By Rudyard Kipling

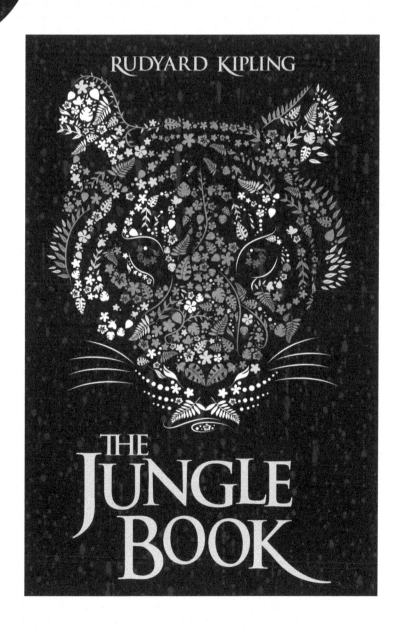

RUDYARD KIPLING

# THE JUNGLE BOOK

# FOR AGES 7–11

Scholastic Education, an imprint of Scholastic Ltd
Book End, Range Road, Witney, Oxfordshire, OX29 0YD
Registered office: Westfield Road, Southam, Warwickshire CV47 0RA

Printed and bound by Ashford Colour Press
© 2018 Scholastic Ltd
1 2 3 4 5 6 7 8 9   8 9 0 1 2 3 4 5 6 7

British Library Cataloguing-in-Publication Data
A catalogue record for this book is available from the British Library.
ISBN 978-1407-18253-7

Extracts from *The National Curriculum in England, English Programme of Study* © Crown Copyright. Reproduced under the terms of the Open Government Licence (OGL). http://www.nationalarchives.gov.uk/doc/open-government-licence/version/3

Due to the nature of the web, we cannot guarantee the content or links of any site mentioned. We strongly recommend that teachers check websites before using them in the classroom.

**Authors** Sarah Snashall
**Editorial team** Rachel Morgan, Vicki Yates, Suzanne Adams, Julia Roberts
**Series designers** Neil Salt and Alice Duggan
**Designer** Alice Duggan
**Illustrator** Mike Phillips/Beehive Illustration

**Acknowledgements**
The publishers gratefully acknowledge permission to reproduce the following copyright material:
**Scholastic Children's Books** for permission to use the cover from *The Jungle Book* written by Rudyard Kipling (Scholastic Children's Books, 2016). Reproduced with permission of Scholastic Children's Books. All rights reserved.

**Photographs**
Page 18: Jungle Book movie poster, Alamy

Every effort has been made to trace copyright holders for the works reproduced in this book, and the publishers apologise for any inadvertent omissions.

# CONTENTS ▼

# How to use Read & Respond in your classroom...

Read & Respond provides teaching ideas related to a specific well-loved children's book. Each Read & Respond book is divided into the following sections:

## ABOUT THE BOOK AND AUTHOR

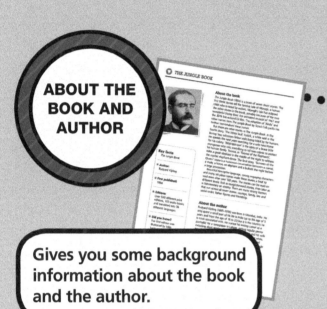

Gives you some background information about the book and the author.

## GUIDED READING

Breaks the book down into sections and gives notes for using it with guided reading groups. A bookmark has been provided on page 12 containing comprehension questions. The children can be directed to refer to these as they read.

## SHARED READING

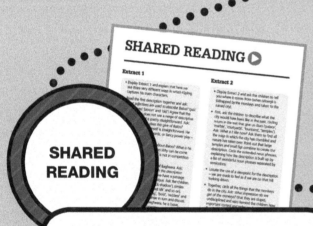

Provides extracts from the children's book with associated notes for focused work. There is also one non-fiction extract that relates to the children's book.

## GRAMMAR, PUNCTUATION & SPELLING

Provides word-level work related to the children's book so you can teach grammar, punctuation and spelling in context.

## PLOT, CHARACTER & SETTING

Contains activity ideas focused on the plot, characters and the setting of the story.

## GET WRITING

Provides writing activities related to the children's book. These activities may be based directly on the children's book or be broadly based on the themes and concepts of the story.

## TALK ABOUT IT

Has speaking and listening activities related to the children's book. These activities may be based directly on the children's book or be broadly based on the themes and concepts of the story.

## ASSESSMENT

Contains short activities that will help you assess whether the children have understood concepts and curriculum objectives. They are designed to be informal activities to feed into your planning.

*❝ The titles are great fun to use and cover exactly the range of books that children most want to read. It makes it easy to explore texts fully and ensure the children want to keep on reading more. ❞*

**Chris Flanagan, Year 5 Teacher,**
**St Thomas of Canterbury**
**Primary School**

## Activities

The activities follow the same format:

- **Objective:** the objective for the lesson. It will be based upon a curriculum objective, but will often be more specific to the focus being covered.

- **What you need:** a list of resources you need to teach the lesson, including photocopiable pages.

- **What to do:** the activity notes.

- **Differentiation:** this is provided where specific and useful differentiation advice can be given to support and/or extend the learning in the activity. Differentiation by providing additional adult support has not been included as this will be at a teacher's discretion based upon specific children's needs and ability, as well as the availability of support.

The activities are numbered for reference within each section and should move through the text sequentially – so you can use the lesson while you are reading the book. Once you have read the book, most of the activities can be used in any order you wish.

# CURRICULUM LINKS

| Section | Activity | Curriculum objectives |
|---|---|---|
| **Guided reading** | | Comprehension: To participate in discussions about books... |
| | | |
| **Shared reading** | 1 | Comprehension: To discuss and evaluate how authors use language, including figurative language, considering the impact on the reader. |
| | 2 | Comprehension: To increase their familiarity with a wide range of books, including... fiction from our literary heritage... |
| | 3 | Comprehension: To draw inferences such as inferring characters' feelings, thoughts and motives from their actions, and justifying inferences with evidence. |
| | 4 | Comprehension: To identify how language, structure and presentation contribute to meaning. |
| | | |
| **Grammar, punctuation & spelling** | 1 | Vocabulary, grammar and punctuation: To use semicolons, colons or dashes to mark boundaries between independent clauses. |
| | 2 | Vocabulary, grammar and punctuation: To recognise vocabulary and structures that are appropriate for formal speech and writing. |
| | 3 | Vocabulary, grammar and punctuation: To punctuate bullet points consistently. |
| | 4 | Vocabulary, grammar and punctuation: To use passive verbs to affect the presentation of information in a sentence. |
| | 5 | Vocabulary, grammar and punctuation: To use and understand the grammatical terminology in English Appendix 2: to understand how words are related by meaning as synonyms and antonyms. |
| | 6 | Spelling: To distinguish between homophones and other words which are often confused. |
| | | |
| **Plot, character & setting** | 1 | Comprehension: To draw inferences such as inferring characters' feelings, thoughts and motives from their actions, and to justify inferences with evidence. |
| | 2 | Comprehension: To summarise the main ideas drawn from more than one paragraph, identifying key details that support main ideas. |
| | 3 | Comprehension: To explain and discuss their understanding of what they have read... |
| | 4 | Comprehension: To discuss and evaluate how authors use language... considering the impact on the reader. |
| | 5 | Comprehension: To make comparisons within and across books. |
| | 6 | Comprehension: To explain and discuss their understanding of what they have read... |
| | 7 | Comprehension: To identify how language, structure and presentation contribute to meaning. |
| | 8 | Vocabulary, grammar and punctuation: To use relative clauses beginning with 'who', 'which', 'where', 'when', 'whose', 'that' or with an implied (i.e. omitted) relative pronoun. |

# CURRICULUM LINKS ▼

| Section | Activity | Curriculum objectives |
|---|---|---|
| **Talk about it** | 1 | Comprehension: To prepare poems... to read aloud... |
| | 2 | Spoken language: To... participate actively in collaborative conversations, staying on topic and initiating and responding to comments. |
| | 3 | Spoken language: To participate in discussions...; to ask relevant questions to extend their understanding and knowledge. |
| | 4 | Comprehension: To identify and discuss themes. |
| | 5 | Spoken language: To participate in... role play [and] improvisation. |
| | 6 | Spoken language: To give well-structured descriptions, explanations and narratives for different purposes, including for expressing feelings. |
| **Get writing** | 1 | Composition: To... select the appropriate form and use other similar writing as models for their own. |
| | 2 | Composition: To select appropriate grammar and vocabulary, understanding how such choices can change and enhance meaning. |
| | 3 | Composition: To draft and write by précising longer passages. |
| | 4 | Composition: To use... organisational and presentational devices to structure text and to guide the reader. |
| | 5 | Composition: In writing narratives, to consider how authors have developed characters and settings in what pupils have read. |
| | 6 | Composition: To perform their own compositions, using appropriate intonation, volume and movement so that meaning is clear. |
| **Assessment** | 1 | Comprehension: To identify and discuss themes and conventions. |
| | 2 | Comprehension: To discuss and evaluate how authors use language, including figurative language, considering the impact on the reader. |
| | 3 | Comprehension: To draw inferences such as inferring characters' motives from their actions, and to justify inferences with evidence. |
| | 4 | Comprehension: To predict what might happen from details stated and implied. |
| | 5 | Comprehension: To increase their familiarity with a wide range of books, including... fiction from our literary heritage... |
| | 6 | Comprehension: To use expanded noun phrases...; to draw inferences such as inferring characters' feelings... and to justify inferences with evidence. |

**READ&RESPOND** The Jungle Book **7**

## Key facts

*The Jungle Book*

◉ **Author:**
Rudyard Kipling

◉ **First published:**
1894

◉ **Editions:**
Over 500 different print editions, 100 audio books and translated into 36 different languages

◉ **Did you know?**
The first edition was illustrated by John Lockwood Kipling, Rudyard Kipling's father.

## About the book

*The Jungle Book* (1894) is a book of seven short stories. The first three stories tell the famous tale of Mowgli, a human child who is raised by wolves. Mowgli's tale has eclipsed the other stories in the book, possibly because of the two wonderful Disney films: the animated musical of 1967 and the 2016 live-action/CGI film. The adoption of 'Akela' and other names from *The Jungle Book* by Scout Cub packs has further immortalised these names.

But there are other stories in *The Jungle Book*. In the fourth story, 'The White Seal', Kotick, a white seal in the Bering Sea, witnesses fellow seals being killed by fur hunters. He spends the next years searching for a safe new home for his colony. 'Rikki-tikki-tavi' is the story of a brave little mongoose who risks everything to kill two cobras to protect his human family. Toomai, in 'Toomai of the Elephants', rides a great elephant in the middle of the night to witness the mythic elephant-dance. The final story, 'Servants of the Queen' reports a humorous conversation between a camel, a mule, a horse, an elephant and a bullock the night before a large procession.

Beautiful descriptive language, strong engaging characters and many set piece scenes make these stories a treat to read even after over 100 years. The stories can be read on different levels: first as straightforward stories, then later as a commentary on society. There are many strong themes that run across all seven stories: courage, family, law and social order, father figures and friendship.

## About the author

Rudyard Kipling (1865–1936) was born in Mumbai, India. He only spent a small part of his life in India (up to the age of 5 years and from the age of 16 to 22) but it is the country he is most associated with. He started his writing career as a journalist for a newspaper in Lahore, writing regular pieces including short stories. After getting married, he and his wife travelled widely before settling in America for a short while. While in America, he wrote *The Jungle Book*, later he returned to England, where he lived for the rest of his life. *The Jungle Book* was a great success and he happily wrote back to children who wrote to him about it. He is also famous for *Just So Stories, Puck of Pook's Hill, The Second Jungle Book, Kim* and the much quoted poem 'If'.

In 1907, Kipling became the first English author to win the Nobel Prize for Literature, but he turned down a knighthood and the post of Poet Laureate.

# GUIDED READING ▶

## Introduction

Introduce the book to the children. Look together at the contents page and explain that this is a collection of seven stories, only the first three of which are about Mowgli. Explain who Rudyard Kipling was and where and when he lived.

## Chapter 1: Mowgli's Brothers

Discuss whether the children have seen either of the films of *The Jungle Book*; if they have, explain that this story is slightly different in places but the main characters are the same, sadly without an appearance by King Louie.

Read the opening, up to the arrival of Shere Khan and his powerful roaring into the cave mouth. Refer to question 11 on the Guided Reading bookmark. Shere Khan has a dramatic build-up and entry. Ask: *What happens when he attacks the woodcutter's camp?* (He misses Mowgli and falls in the fire.) Agree that Shere Khan is an angry fool. Compare this to the arrival of Mowgli, asking volunteers to locate the passage: 'He is altogether without hair, and I could kill him with a touch of my foot. But see, he looks up and is not afraid.' Mowgli enters the story bravely, unlike Shere Khan. It is clear from the outset who will win this battle.

Read about the first meeting on the Council Rock, from 'There was very little talking…' Ask: *Why does each named member of the Pack agree to take in Mowgli?* (Baloo sees no harm; Bagheera sees potential power; Mother Wolf has maternal instinct and wants to protect him from Shere Khan.) Ask: *How do the wolves organise themselves?* (They have a chosen leader, formal meetings, a clear way of behaving and strict rules about how someone can join the pack.)

Move on to focus on the section that begins, 'Now you must be content to skip ten or eleven whole years', and describes Mowgli's idyllic life in the jungle. Ask: *How does Mowgli's life in the jungle sound?* Read the first page of this section, picking out the details. Refer to question 10 on the bookmark, encouraging the children to see how the layers of small detail create the larger setting. Discuss the Law of the Jungle. Ask: *What does Mowgli learn about the Jungle?* (The rules allow the animals to live with each other.)

Read the second meeting at the Council Rock, from 'Akela the Lone Wolf lay by the side of his rock…' Ask: *What has happened to the Pack?* (Shere Khan has divided it.) *What is the ultimate power?* (Mowgli with the red flower – the symbol of being a man.) Ask: *Why does the Pack cast him out?*

## Chapter 2: Kaa's Hunting

Read the first half of this chapter up to the point where Kaa agrees to fight with Baloo and Bagheera. ('All one. Let us go on…') Ask: *When does this chapter take place?* Agree that it has gone back to the idyllic time when Mowgli was taught by Baloo. Ask: *What sort of teacher is Baloo?* (quite strict but a good teacher) Ask: *What sort of student is Mowgli?* (an excellent one) Ask volunteers to find examples of what Mowgli learns and why. Ask: *Why does Baloo beat Mowgli?* (to make him learn, though Bagheera does not agree with this) *What do Baloo and Bagheera think of Mowgli?* (They love him dearly.)

Ask: *How has Mowgli met the Monkey People?* (They came to him after a beating and promised him he could be their leader.) *Should Mowgli trust them?* Ask volunteers to read Baloo's woeful declarations of self-pity when Mowgli is stolen. Ask: *How does Bagheera persuade Kaa to fight for them?* (through flattery and by telling him that the monkeys have insulted him)

# GUIDED READING

Read up to the paragraph ending 'But I am tired...' Refer to question 1 on the bookmark. Recap on the Law of the Jungle and compare this with how the monkeys behave. Enjoy the description of the Cold Lairs, noting favourite noun phrases. Read to the end of the chapter and ask volunteers to explain what happens in the fight. Ask: *How is it won?* (by Kaa hypnotising the monkeys – and probably eating them) Ask: *Why does Mowgli give such fulsome thanks to Kaa?* (He has been taught well and knows that Kaa could easily eat him another day.) Compare his behaviour towards Kaa with his behaviour towards Shere Khan.

## Chapter 3: Tiger! Tiger!

Read the poem at the start of this chapter together. Refer to question 8 on the bookmark. Discuss how the poems are a mixture of commentary, summary or celebration of the stories. Agree that here it is a comment on Akela growing old.

Read the opening of this chapter up to Mowgli leaving the village meeting ('...Buldeo puffed and snorted at Mowgli's impertinence.') Ask: *When does this chapter take place?* Refer to question 6 on the bookmark and ask a volunteer to describe the story of Mowgli in chronological order. Remember why Mowgli was cast out of the Pack. Ask: *How do you think he will get on with humans? What problems will he have? Who is in charge of the village? How does he behave?* (The priest is in charge: he places Mowgli with a rich lady in order to gain favour.) Point out that power games are afoot here as well as in the Pack. Ask: *What does Mowgli think of the humans?* (That they are as silly and vain as the monkeys.)

Read to the end of the chapter. Ask: *How does Mowgli kill Shere Khan?* Point out that he uses Shere Khan's own stupidity, teamwork and his own cunning. Ask: *Why does Buldeo want to steal the hide? (so he can get a reward for killing Shere Khan)*

Ask question 2 on the bookmark and discuss how both wolves and humans are afraid of Mowgli. Ask: *What do you predict for Mowgli's future?* Discuss his power over fire, his cunning and leadership. Discuss the impact of him wearing Shere Khan's hide. Ask: *Are you pleased that he stayed in the jungle at the end (for the time being)?*

## Chapter 4: The White Seal

Explain that the lullaby at the beginning sets the theme of family life and safety in this story. This is a myth-style quest story that fits into the tradition of stories that describe the journey to a new safer land (another example being *Watership Down* by Richard Adams). In these stories one brave individual (here a white seal) saves a nation.

Read up to the point where Kotick sees seals being killed. Ask: *How does this fit in with the Law of the Jungle?* (Seals have their own structure of society, as do the wolves.) Refer to question 15 on the bookmark. Ask: *Are the men wrong to kill seals?* Refer to question 3 on the bookmark and discuss the reasons for leaving the island. Ask: *Why are the other seals happy to stay?*

Focus on the description of the idyllic new home (a real promised land). Ask: *Where will the different parts of the colony live?* Ask the children if they can think of another journey to a secret location in this book. (Mowgli and the Cold Lairs, and later on, Toomai and the elephant dance.)

Ask question 9 on the bookmark and point out that this story is not set in the jungle, asking the children to think of reasons for its inclusion. (It is a story about animals; it matches the theme of animals living together.)

## Chapter 5: Rikki-Tikki-Tavi

The story of Rikki-tikki-tavi is like a Chinese myth where a person who helps someone or something (that looks inconspicuous but turns out to be a fairy) is then helped in return. This is the story of a mongoose who is saved by a family, who in turn saves the family from three snakes in a series of clever and daring trials, not unlike the 'risk all' sequences of an action film.

Read up to Rikki-tikki's encounter with Nag. Ask: *Why is Nag scarier than Shere Khan?* (He is not a fool.) Ask question 12 on the bookmark, encouraging the children to capture Rikki-tikki's busy nature, his cute appearance and his fierce personality. Read to the end of the story. Ask the children to list the times Rikki-tikki saves the family: by killing Karait, by killing Nag, by distracting Nagaina, by destroying the eggs and by killing Nagaina. Enjoy the chorus of the animals in the garden. Ask: *Why does Rikki-tikki risk all?* (character, loyalty, instinct) *How do the other animals help him?*

## Chapter 6: Toomai of the Elephants

Read up to the point where Toomai meets Petersen Sahib. Ask: *What is the situation here?* (Petersen catches elephants and they form a working herd.) Point out that in this story, the animals are not free, but are captured from the forest – they are also the only animals whose speech is not reported in *The Jungle Book*. Refer again to question 15 on the bookmark. Discuss the issue here, and then again at the end of the story.

Focus on the elephant-dance. Point out that this climactic scene is described only through sound and feeling. Ask question 14 on the bookmark. Agree that describing a scene using only sound creates atmosphere, makes it seem very mysterious and focuses the attention on the incredible sound the elephants make.

## Chapter 7: Servants of the Queen

In this story, a group of animals in the Indian army discuss their role in battle. Read the story together, doing different voices if possible. Refer to question 5 on the bookmark. (A camel who has had a nightmare has knocked the tent over and become entangled with it.) Ask: *Why is Two Tails scared of the fighting?* Ask question 16 on the bookmark. Encourage the children to find the role each animal has in battle and see how these fit together.

## Final thoughts

Ask the children to share their final thoughts about *The Jungle Book*. Ask: *What was your favourite story?* Ask question 13 on the bookmark. Listen to the children's suggestions and share your thoughts, for example Shere Khan at the mouth of the cave, the Cold Lairs, Kotick finding the hidden beaches, the elephant-dance. Ask question 17 on the bookmark. Agree that they are children's stories. Ask: *What makes them children's stories?* (talking animals, simple vocabulary) Ask: *Might adults enjoy them?* Point out that they have interesting themes and beautiful language that will be enjoyed by everyone.

## The Jungle Book
### by Rudyard Kipling

### Focus on...
### Meaning

1. Why do the Jungle People hate the Monkey People?
2. Why is Mowgli cast out by the wolves and the humans?
3. Why does Kotick want to find a new home?
4. What is the meaning of the elephant-dance?
5. What happens to the narrator's tent?

---

### Focus on...
### Organisation

6. Describe the timeline of Mowgli's story.
7. Name three stories where the characters travel to a secret location.
8. What do the poems add to the stories?
9. Does the story of 'The White Seal' fit in *The Jungle Book*?

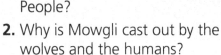

## The Jungle Book
### by Rudyard Kipling

### Focus on...
### Language and features

10. How does Kipling create setting?
11. How does Kipling create the character of Shere Khan?
12. Describe Rikki-tikki-tavi.
13. What scenes from *The Jungle Book* stand out for you?

---

### Focus on...
### Purpose, viewpoints and effects

14. What is the effect of describing a scene through sound only?
15. Does Kipling think that humans treat animals well?
16. How does 'Servants of the Queen' develop the theme of teamwork?
17. Who were these stories written for?

# SHARED READING ▶

## Extract 1

- Display Extract 1 and explain that here we see three very different ways in which Kipling captures his main characters.

- Read the first description together and ask: *What adjectives are used to describe Baloo?* (just 'sleepy' and 'brown' and 'old') Agree that this introduction does not use a range of descriptive techniques and is pretty straightforward. Ask: *What impression does this give of Baloo?* (Perhaps that he himself is straightforward. He does not use fancy words, or fancy power play – he speaks the truth.)

- Ask: *What do we learn about Baloo? What is his place in the Pack?* (teacher) *Why can he come and go as he pleases?* (He is not in competition with the wolves for food.)

- Now read the description of Bagheera. Ask: *How does this contrast with the description of Baloo?* Agree that here we have a passage dripping with literary technique. Ask the children to locate a metaphor ('black shadow'), similes ('like the pattern of watered silk' and so on), adjectives galore ('cunning', 'bold', 'reckless' and so on). Focus on each simile in turn and discuss what it tells us about Bagheera: he is brave, clever and a smooth operator.

- Move on to focus on Mowgli. Point out that here, Kipling describes not Mowgli himself but what he does, and this is equally effective. Together circle all the verbs. Ask: *What is Mowgli doing? How does he behave?* (He is singeing the wolves; he is quick and decisive.) *Then what happens?* (He cries.) *Why?* (for the loss of the Pack) *What do we learn about Mowgli?* (He is filled with emotion: first righteous fury, then sorrow.)

## Extract 2

- Display Extract 2 and ask the children to tell you where it comes from (when Mowgli is kidnapped by the monkeys and taken to the ruined city).

- First, ask the children to describe what the city would have been like in the past, circling nouns in the text that give us clues ('palace', 'marble', 'courtyards', 'fountains', 'temples'). Ask: *What is it like now?* Ask them to find all the ways in which the city has crumbled and nature has taken over. Point out that large temples and small figs combine to create the description. Circle the extended noun phrases, explaining how the description is built up by a list of wonderful noun phrases separated by semicolons.

- Locate the use of a viewpoint for the description – we are made to feel as if we are on that hill looking down.

- Together, circle all the things that the monkeys do in the city. Ask: *What impression do we get of the monkeys?* (that they are stupid, undisciplined and vain) Remind the children how important control and order are for the Jungle People. Find Baloo's description of the monkeys as 'evil, dirty, shameless' with a 'desire… to be noticed by the Jungle People'. Ask: *Is he right in his assessment?*

- Ask: *What do the monkeys say of themselves? Are they right?* Compare the monkeys' desire to be like man with their undignified behaviour pretending to be human in a crumbled city that they don't understand.

## Extract 3

- Display Extract 3, the climax of 'Toomai of the Elephants'. Ask the children to remember what has come before.

- Ask: *What can Toomai see in this extract?* (nothing) *What is being described?* (what he can hear) *What is the effect of this?* (creates atmosphere; makes it more scary for Toomai; keeps the secret of the elephant-dance which Toomai only experiences and doesn't really see)

- Together, circle the sounds that Toomai can hear. Ask: *How do the sounds change?* Agree that they get louder and louder: first they are quiet rustling and gurgling sounds, then silence, then a sudden and almighty trumpet, then stamping and crashing that is so loud that Toomai can feel it in his body. Encourage the children to imagine if this scene was filmed – what would the soundtrack be like? Introduce the word 'crescendo', meaning getting louder. Remind the children of previous descriptive passages with layers of detail.

- Ask: *What does Toomai feel physically?* He can feel the dew, the motion of the elephants, the noise through his body. Imagine the sudden shock of the trunk touching his knee in the dark.

- Ask: *What does Toomai feel emotionally?* (perhaps scared and shocked, but also elated)

- Ask: *Why does Toomai feel as if he is alone, when he is surrounded by elephants?* (He is the only human, he is not part of the dance, he cannot see anything.)

- Ask: *Without any description of what can be seen, can you describe what happens in the elephant-dance?*

## Extract 4

- If possible, watch the 2016 film of *The Jungle Book* before sharing Extract 4. After reading a book steeped in myth and imagination, the facts of the creation of *The Jungle Book* film almost seem the most unbelievable story. Support this text by watching clips of Neel Sethi on the Disney sound stage and of the way the animation of the animals was built up.

- Ask: *What sort of text is this?* (explanation) *What features can we find?* Circle the elements as the children find them: title, subtitle, adverbials for time ('First', 'then', 'finally'), description of a process, technical terms, did you know box.

- Ask: *What rhetorical features can we spot?* (questions; emotive language such as 'unimaginable', 'breathtaking', 'impact')

- Ask: *What technical terms are specific to this subject – the film industry?* Discuss the meaning of each. ('live action' – filmed with real people; 'motion capture' – recording the movement of an animal or person in order to animate a character; 'frame' – a picture that is combined with thousands of pictures to make a film; 'sound stage' – a stage used in filming)

- Ask: *Does this non-fiction text have a point of view?* Agree that it tries to persuade you to admire the skill and success of the film. Ask: *Does it make you want to watch the film/watch it again?*

# Extract 1

### Baloo

Then… Baloo, the sleepy brown bear who teaches the wolf cubs the Law of the Jungle; old Baloo, who can come and go where he pleases because he eats only nuts and roots and honey – rose up on his hind quarters and grunted.

"The man's cub – the man's cub?" he said. "*I* speak for the man's cub. There is no harm in a man's cub. I have no gift of words, but I speak the truth. Let him run with the Pack, and be entered with the others. I myself will teach him."

### Bagheera

A black shadow dropped down into the circle. It was Bagheera, the Black Panther, inky black all over, but with the panther markings showing up in certain lights like the pattern of watered silk. Everybody knew Bagheera, and nobody cared to cross his path; for he was as cunning as Tabaqui, as bold as the wild buffalo, and as reckless as the wounded elephant. But he had a voice as soft as wild honey dripping from a tree, and a skin softer than down.

### Mowgli

The fire was burning furiously at the end of the branch, and Mowgli struck right and left round the circle, and the wolves ran howling with the sparks burning their fur. At last there were only Akela, Bagheera and perhaps ten wolves that had taken Mowgli's part. Then something began to hurt Mowgli inside him, as he had never been hurt in his life before, and he caught his breath and sobbed, and the tears ran down his face.

# Extract 2

A great roofless palace crowned the hill, and the marble of the courtyards and the fountains was split and stained with red and green, and the very cobblestones in the courtyard where the king's elephants used to live had been thrust up and apart by grasses and young trees. From the palace you could see the rows and rows of roofless houses that made up the city, looking like empty honeycombs filled with blackness; the shapeless block of stone that had been an idol, in the square where four roads met; the pits and dimples at street-corners where the public wells once stood; and the shattered domes of temples with wild figs sprouting on their sides.

The monkeys called the place their city, and pretended to despise the Jungle People because they lived in the forest. And yet they never knew what the buildings were made for nor how to use them. They would sit in circles on the hall of the king's council chamber, and scratch for fleas and pretend to be men; or they would run in and out of the roofless houses and collect pieces of plaster and old bricks in a corner, and forget where they had hidden them, and fight and cry in scuffling crowds, and then break off to play up and down the terraces of the king's garden, where they would shake the rose-trees and the oranges in sport to see the fruit and flowers fall… they would all rush together in mobs and shout: "There are none in the jungle so wise and good and clever and strong and gentle as the *Bandar-log*." Then all would begin again till they grew tired of the city and went back to the tree-tops, hoping the Jungle People would notice them.

# Extract 3

Then a cloud came over the moon, and he sat in black darkness; but the quiet, steady hustling and pushing and gurgling went on just the same. He knew that there were elephants all round Kala Nag, and that there was no chance of backing him out of the assembly; so he set his teeth and shivered. In a Keddah at least there was torch-light and shouting, but here he was all alone in the dark, and once a trunk came up and touched him on the knee.

Then an elephant trumpeted, and they all took it up for five or ten terrible seconds. The dew from the trees above spattered down like rain on the unseen backs, and a dull booming noise began, not very loud at first, and Little Toomai could not tell what it was; but it grew and grew, and Kala Nag lifted up one fore-foot and then the other, and brought them down on the ground – one – two, one – two, as steadily as trip-hammers. The elephants were stamping altogether now, and it sounded like a war-drum beaten at the mouth of a cave. The dew fell from the trees till there was no more left to fall, and the booming went on, and the ground rocked and shivered, and Little Toomai put his hands up to his ears to shut out the sound. But it was all one gigantic jar that ran through him – this stamp of hundreds of heavy feet on the raw earth. Once or twice he could feel Kala Nag and all the others surge forward a few strides, and the thumping would change to the crushing sound of juicy green things being bruised, but in a minute or two the boom of feet on hard earth began again.

# Extract 4

### Bringing *The Jungle Book* to life

In 2016, Disney produced a new *The Jungle Book* film to complement its original 1967 animated musical. What was different about this film? For a start it was more sophisticated, closer to the original book and scarier. It was also filmed as live action – or was it? Believe it or not, apart from Mowgli, played by Neel Sethi, *The Jungle Book* (2016) is almost entirely animated. How did they do it?

### New technology

Director Jon Favreau used new animation technology that combined the techniques of live action, motion capture and animation. Actor Neel Sethi, who plays Mowgli, acted on a rotating stage against a blue background. Actors in blue suits walked alongside him, carried him and threw shadows on him. Animators then added in the background and the talking animals.

### Research, research, research

The animators spent hours – weeks – months – researching the animals in the movie and how they would move. Particular work was done ensuring that any mouth movement for talking matched the way that particular animal moved its mouth. First, a skeleton of the animal was animated, then muscles were added and, finally, the fur that moves and catches the light.

### Dedication

Each frame of the movie took 20 to 30 hours to complete – and it takes 24 frames to make one second of the film. That's an almost unimaginable amount of work, but the result was a movie of breathtaking impact that allows the audience to lose themselves in the world of *The Jungle Book*.

# GRAMMAR, PUNCTUATION & SPELLING ▶

## 1. Using dashes

### Objective
To use semicolons, colons or dashes to mark boundaries between independent clauses.

### What you need
Copies of *The Jungle Book*.

### What to do
- As a class, locate instances in the first five pages of *The Jungle Book* where Kipling uses a dash. Agree the purpose of each (for parenthesis, emphasis, or to divide clauses).

- Ask pairs to continue looking though 'Mowgli's Brothers' to find three sentences that use one or more dashes.

- Ask volunteers to write one of their sentences on the board and to underline the clause that has been introduced by the dash. Together, decide what job the dash (or dashes) does and discuss different punctuation marks that could have been used instead. For example: a pair of commas or brackets (for parenthesis), ellipsis (break in speech), or semicolon or colon (independent clause).

- Ask the pairs to write out the three sentences they have chosen using different punctuation.

- Discuss the flexibility of the dash as a punctuation mark, versus the more precise nature of the colon, semicolon and brackets.

### Differentiation
**Support:** Provide children with a range of straightforward sentences where the dash could be replaced with a semicolon or a colon.

**Extension:** Ecourage children to discuss trickier sentences in the story. For example, discuss alternative ways of punctuating 'Chattering, foolish, vain – vain, foolish and chattering – are monkeys.'

## 2. Formal speech

### Objective
To recognise vocabulary and structures that are appropriate for formal speech and writing.

### What you need
Copies of *The Jungle Book*.

### What to do
- Re-read together the events at two Wolf councils in 'Mowgli's Brothers'.

- Clarify any misapprehension regarding 'thou' and 'thee' (old-fashioned, but informal versions of 'you'; 'ye' being the formal or plural version).

- Ask the children, in pairs, to note down formal phrases from these meetings, for example, repetition: 'Who speaks… who speaks'; formal politeness: 'O Akela… I have no right'; impersonal tone: 'none can hope'; formal syntax: 'We need yet another'.

- Afterwards, share ideas about why the characters speak the way they do. (For example, Akela and Bagheera to show authority and make formal arguments; the Pack shows how disrespectful it is as it acts like a crowd shouting someone down.)

- Ask the children to work in groups to read aloud each council meeting, bringing out the contrast between Akela and Bagheera on one hand and the Pack and Shere Khan on the other.

### Differentiation
**Extension:** Ask: *What does this use of language add to the story?* (For example, it shows character and purpose, it adds atmosphere.)

## 3. Bullet points

**Objective**

To punctuate bullet points consistently.

**What you need**

Copies of *The Jungle Book*.

**What to do**

- Together, create a list of conventions for bullet lists. For example:
  1. Introduce the bullet list with a colon.
  2. Choose capital letters, semicolons, full stops or no punctuation, as appropriate, but be consistent.
  3. Use a similar style for each bullet: all sentences, all one word, all in the present tense, all in the past tense, all starting with a verb, and so on.

- Use the list of places Kotick visits in 'The White Seal', or the things Mowgli learns about the jungle in 'Mowgli's Brothers' (the paragraph starting 'Now you must be content') to model writing a bulleted list.

- Organise the children in groups to create a series of lists about *The Jungle Book*. (For example, favourite scenes, main characters, themes, list of stories, adjectives to describe Bagheera, settings and so on.) Encourage them to write some lists comprising sentences or phrases.

- Ask the children to work individually to write down two or three bulleted lists, using the conventions discussed.

**Differentiation**

**Support:** Ask children to list the main five characters, with a brief description (such as Mowgli, a boy brought up by the wolves) so that they can focus their time on creating consistent bullet point lists.

**Extension:** Challenge children to find some of the descriptive lists Kipling uses in the book and turn them into bullet point lists.

## 4. Practising passive

**Objective**

To use passive verbs to affect the presentation of information in a sentence.

**What you need**

Copies of *The Jungle Book*, photocopiable page 22 'Practising the passive'.

**What to do**

- Write a short passage on the board comprising one active and one passive sentence, for example: 'The cobra, Nag, was defeated at last by the brave mongoose. It lay, still and silent, on the bathroom floor'.

- Ask the children to say which sentence is active and which is passive. (Point out that the second sentence is active even though the cobra is dead!)

- Recap on the difference between active and passive verbs using a range of matching sentences, for example: 'Shere Khan <u>stole</u> the baby. The baby <u>was stolen</u> by Shere Khan.'; 'Baloo <u>taught</u> Mowgli and the other cubs. Mowgli and the other cubs <u>were taught</u> by Baloo.'

- Hand out photocopiable page 22 'Practising the passive' and ask the children to carry out the activity individually. Afterwards, ask them to compare their answers with a partner, correcting any mistakes.

- Challenge the children, still working in their pairs, to create pairs of matching active and passive sentences related to *The Jungle Book*, taking turns to create an active sentence for their partner to turn into the passive voice. If they are struggling with ideas, encourage them to flick through *The Jungle Book* for inspiration.

**Differentiation**

**Support:** Give the children three or more passive sentences and ask them to make the sentences active.

**Extension:** Challenge children to write descriptions comprising two sentences: one active and one passive.

# 5. Finding synonyms

### Objective
To understand how words are related by meaning as synonyms and antonyms.

### What you need
Photocopiable page 23 'Finding synonyms'; copies of *The Jungle Book*.

### What to do

• Agree that although *The Jungle Book* was written over 100 years ago, the vocabulary is usually familiar. Point out that Kipling creates great effects with straightforward vocabulary: sometimes by using a surprising word; sometimes by using the perfect word.

• Write the following quotations on the board: (from 'The White Seal') 'he was all but smashed to pieces against some wicked black cliffs', and (from 'Mowgli's Brothers') 'Mother Wolf… sprang forward, her eyes, like two green moons in the darkness, facing the blazing eyes of Shere Khan.' Underline the words 'smashed', 'wicked', 'moons' and 'blazing'. Together, try out synonyms in their place such as 'broken', 'dangerous', 'discs', 'furious' and so on. Discuss the effect.

• Ask the children to complete photocopiable page 23 'Finding synonyms', working in pairs for the discussion part.

• Try out the different synonyms that the children have chosen. Discuss the different options, for example: 'pushed' might not have the power behind it that 'thrust' does – perhaps 'shoved' might work better. Point out that 'terrible' describes not the noise but the waiting – perhaps 'nail-biting' or 'painful' might be suitable synonyms.

### Differentiation
**Support:** Provide word cards for children to choose from ('shoved', 'forced', 'exploring', 'wandering', 'awful', 'clumsy', 'cries', 'moans').

**Extension:** Ask children to articulate the deeper meaning of the underlined words, for example 'blundering' means a combination of staggering blindly and stupidly.

# 6. Checking homophones

### Objective
To spell homophones and other words that are often confused.

### What you need
Copies of *The Jungle Book*, photocopiable page 24 'Checking homophones', photocopiable page 42 'Lazy jungle life' (optional).

### What to do

• Begin by revising homophones (words with the same sound but different meanings and spellings).

• On the board, write the following words: 'roar', 'eight', 'groan', 'son', 'hole', 'meet' and 'clause'. Locate the paragraph that starts the third section of 'Mowgli's Brothers' (from 'Now you must be content to skip…' – if preferred, you could display the text as it appears on photocopiable page 42 'Lazy jungle life'). Read the paragraph together as a class, finding a homophone for each word on the board. Discuss the different meanings of the homophones.

• Encourage pairs to work together to create a sentence for each word on the board.

• Then ask the children to complete photocopiable page 24 'Checking homophones' individually.

• Share the sentences for each word, discussing ways to remember which spelling is which, for example, 'farther' has the word 'far' in it (and 'father' unfortunately has 'fat'), 'passed' and 'guessed' are verbs, 'wary' rhymes with 'scary', when writing 'who's' check that you can replace it with 'who is' and so on.

### Differentiation
**Support:** Ask children to create fewer sentences from the words on the board.

**Extension:** Challenge children to tackle other passages from the book in the same way, identifying homophones for words in the book and using them in new sentences.

 # Practising the passive

- Read each sentence and tick the correct box to show if it is 'active' or 'passive'.

- Then underline the verb (or verbs) in each one.

**1.** The monkeys kidnapped Mowgli.  **Active** ☐  **Passive** ☐

**2.** Shere Khan was trampled to death by the cattle.  **Active** ☐  **Passive** ☐

**3.** Rikki-tikki-tavi followed Nagaina down the hole.  **Active** ☐  **Passive** ☐

**4.** Kotick was bobbed up and down by the waves.  **Active** ☐  **Passive** ☐

**5.** The tent was destroyed by the stampeding camels.  **Active** ☐  **Passive** ☐

**6.** Toomai watched as the elephants danced.  **Active** ☐  **Passive** ☐

- The sentences below are in the active. Rewrite them so that they are in the passive.

**1.** Kotick found a safe place for the seal colony.

_____

_____

**2.** The wolf pack surrounded Akela.

_____

_____

**3.** The monkeys dragged Mowgli into the Cold Lairs.

_____

_____

**4.** Vixen frightened Two Tails by yapping at him.

_____

_____

**5.** Kotick led an army of ten thousand seals through the Sea Cow's tunnel to safety.

_____

_____

# Finding synonyms

- Use a thesaurus to find a synonym for the underlined word in each sentence.

- Discuss whether you prefer your word or Kipling's.

- Write a sentence of your own using the underlined word.

**1.** The very cobblestones had been **thrust** up and apart by grasses and young trees.

**Synonym:** _____

_____

_____

**2.** Rikki-tikki… spent all that day **roaming** over the house.

**Synonym:** _____

_____

_____

**3.** Then an elephant trumpeted, and they all took it up for five or ten **terrible** seconds.

**Synonym:** _____

_____

_____

**4.** "You big, **blundering** beast of a camel you, you upset our tent!"

**Synonym:** _____

_____

_____

**5.** Chuchundra… **whimpers** and cheeps all the night, trying to make up his mind to run into the middle of the room; but he never gets there.

**Synonym:** _____

_____

_____

# Checking homophones

● Choose and write the correct spelling for the missing word in each sentence.

1. (Farther / Father) _____ Wolf and Mother Wolf took Mowgli to the council meeting.

2. (heard / herd) The Wolves _____ Shere Khan howling in anger.

3. (morning / mourning) In the _____, Toomai could see that the elephants had trampled down many trees.

4. (passed / past) In the _____, Akela had fallen into three different traps.

5. (steel / steal) Mowgli crept up to the villager's house in order to _____ a pot of fire.

6. (wary / weary) Two Tails was _____ of going too close to the sound of battle.

7. (who's / whose) Mowgli went to live with Messua, _____ own son had been taken by Shere Khan.

8. (farther / father) Mowgli walked 20 miles to a village much _____ down the valley.

9. (heard / herd) Akela frightened the _____ and they charged down the ravine.

10. (Who's / Whose) " _____ willing to speak for this man-cub?" asked Akela.

# PLOT, CHARACTER & SETTING ▶

## 1. The baby in the jungle

### Objective
To draw inferences such as inferring characters' feelings, thoughts and motives, and to justify inferences with evidence.

### What you need
Copies of *The Jungle Book*.

### What to do

- Read the opening of *The Jungle Book* together, up to the entrance of the baby Mowgli. Ask: *What has happened to Mowgli up to this point? Where has he been? How do we know?*

- Together, find the clues in the text about the events that are happening 'off stage' (the sounds the wolves can hear in the distance, the reports of Shere Khan's jump).

- Ask: *Why has Kipling written it this way?* (for drama; to create the surprise of Mowgli arriving; because the reader never sees the story from Shere Khan's point of view)

- Tell the children to write the scene where Mowgli is separated from his parents, using the facts they know and adding in inferred events (the woodcutter and family running in panic, calling to each other) and feelings (their fear at the tiger – they run away; Mowgli's lack of fear). Ask: *Why does Shere Khan want Mowgli? How do the parents feel when they realise Mowgli is missing?*

- Tell the children to end their passage with Mowgli toddling through the thicket towards the wolves.

### Differentiation

**Support:** Ask children to infer the events of the scene and discuss them with others. They should then role play the events rather than writing them down.

**Extension:** Ensure children are writing a cohesive passage, with sections and sentences linked using a range of devices.

## 2. Shadow theatres

### Objective
To summarise the main ideas drawn from more than one paragraph.

### What you need
Copies of *The Jungle Book*, photocopiable page 29 'Shadow puppets'.

### Cross-curricular links
Art and design, drama

### What to do

- Read the opening of *The Jungle Book* from the point at which Mowgli arrives at the cave of the wolves until Mowgli's acceptance into the Pack.

- Ask: *What are the key events in this section?* Ask pairs to list six to eight events, for example: 1. The arrival of Tabaqui, 2. Hearing Shere Khan in the distance, 3. The arrival of Mowgli, 4. The arrival of Shere Khan at the mouth of the cave, 5. Going to the Council Rock, 6. Bagheera and Baloo speaking for Mowgli, 7. Mowgli being accepted.

- Ask pairs to write a dramatic sentence for each event, using ideas and vocabulary from the book.

- Provide pairs with photocopiable page 29 'Shadow puppets' and ask them to use the templates to create shadow puppets using card and craft sticks. Children then use their puppets to create a shadow puppet version of their opening, practising it ready for performance.

- Set up a light and sheet and ask pairs to perform their puppet shows to the class.

### Differentiation

**Support:** Provide children with a series of statements to order, then use these for their story.

**Extension:** Challenge children to use the best language, using pauses and sound effects to create a great performance.

# PLOT, CHARACTER & SETTING

## 3. Mowgli, the man-cub

> **Objective**
> To explain and discuss their understanding of what they have read.
>
> **What you need**
> Copies of *The Jungle Book*, large pieces of paper.

**What to do**

- After reading the first three chapters, ask: *What is Mowgli like?* With each adjective that a child suggests, encourage them to relate the description to a particular event in the story.

- After sharing a few suggestions, ask the children to work in pairs to create a list of adjectives for Mowgli, with evidence from the text. For example: 'brave' (he walks into the wolves' lair smiling), 'clever' (he learns the animal and human words quickly), 'vain' (he is flattered by the monkeys), 'fun-loving' (he enjoys being swung through the trees), 'fierce' (he attacks Shere Khan and his followers with fire), 'cunning' (he traps and kills Shere Khan), 'loveable' (Bagheera, Baloo and Mother Wolf all love him fiercely), 'polite' (he is polite to Chil, to Kaa and to the snakes in the pit), 'part-wolf' (follows the laws of the wolves), 'part-man' (can weave and use fire).

- Ask the children to draw an annotated picture of Mowgli; tell them to draw Mowgli in the centre and surround him with sentences that use the adjectives they've collected.

> **Differentiation**
> **Support:** Provide children with adjectives for Mowgli (as suggested above) and examples on slips of paper. Ask them to match the adjectives with the evidence and stick them onto their picture.
>
> **Extension:** Encourage children to move on do the same activity for Kotick and Toomai. When they have finished, encourage them to compare the characters.

## 4. Battle of the Cats

> **Objective**
> To discuss and evaluate how authors use language, considering the impact on the reader.
>
> **What you need**
> Copies of *The Jungle Book*, photocopiable page 30 'Battle of the cats'.

**What to do**

- Read the scene where Shere Khan roars through the mouth of the cave. Ask: *How does this scene make you feel? (scared, apprehensive, annoyed, upset)*

- Together create a list of adjectives for Shere Khan, separating them into 'scary' and 'not scary' such as 'powerful', 'lame', 'cunning', 'obsessed', 'manipulative', 'clever'.

- Ask pairs to hunt for the names Shere Khan is called, for example: 'the Big One', 'Lungri' (the 'Lame One'), 'My Lord', 'striped cattle-killer', 'frog-eater', 'fish-killer', 'singed jungle-cat' and so on. Add these to the board.

- Ask the pairs again to find longer lines about Shere Khan, such as: 'Fool Fool!… Eaten and drunk too', 'all long tail and loud talk like Mor the Peacock', 'whimpered and whined', 'He has missed'. Now search for descriptions of Bagheera, for example at the Council Rock, watching Mowgli, admiring his 'steel-blue, ripping-chisel talons', fighting the monkeys and so on.

- Provide the children with photocopiable page 30 'Battle of the cats' and ask them to write descriptions of the two cats, drawing on vocabulary from the book.

> **Differentiation**
> **Support:** Provide the children with the names, adjectives and quotations on cards. Use the cards to start a discussion in pairs about the two cats.
>
> **Extension:** Challenge the children to focus on comparing the two cats (Bagheera has chosen Mowgli because he sees his potential power while Shere Khan whispers into the ears of the young wolves; Bagheera has Baloo while Shere Khan has Tabaqui).

# 5. Jungle boy; village boy

## Objective
To make comparisons within books.

## What you need
Copies of *The Jungle Book*.

## Cross-curricular link
Geography

## What to do

- Together, read the two paragraphs in 'Mowgli's Brothers' beginning 'Now you must be content to skip ten or eleven whole years…' Focus on the phrases that repeat 'every…' Admire Kipling's skill in building up the setting and lazy atmosphere. Ask the children to find the animal words. Discuss how a setting is created both by the landscape and its inhabitants.

- Ask pairs to create a mind map about the jungle. Encourage them to look at 'Mowgli's Brothers' and 'Kaa's Hunting' for inspiration, noting down details about the contrasting settings (the main jungle and the Cold Lairs) and animals (the loyal and friendly animals in comparison to the evil Shere Khan, the naughty monkeys, the scary Kaa and so on). Encourage them to add related quotations and an indication of character and emotion when they can be inferred (for example the insecure monkeys and the vain python).

- Ask the children to now turn to 'Tiger! Tiger!' and, again in discussion with a partner, create a mind map for the village and the people in it. Ask them to create annotated circles about the inside of the house, how Mowgli feels and the different people in the village, and what they think about Mowgli.

## Differentiation
**Support:** Provide partially completed mind maps and let them work together as a group to complete the maps.

**Extension:** Expect children to create more sophisticated mind maps that indicate contrasting feelings and relationships.

# 6. A little piece of heaven

## Objective
To explain and discuss their understanding of what they have read.

## What you need
Images of St Paul's Island, Alaska and the seals that live there; copies of *The Jungle Book*; art materials.

## Cross-curricular link
Art and design

## What to do

- Look together at the images of St Paul's Island, Alaska, and the seals that live there. Look at the landscape around the seals in the images.

- Re-read the opening of 'The White Seal', locating together who lives where (the families, the bachelors and the young seals).

- Ask pairs to find and re-read the description of the land beyond the tunnel – another one of Kipling's great lists. Ask the children to locate expanded noun phrases used, such as, 'long stretches of smooth-worn rock running for miles, exactly fitted to make seal-nurseries', 'delightful low sandy islands half hidden in the beautiful rolling fog'.

- Encourage the children to draw or paint a picture of Kotick's secret, perfect new home, annotating it with noun phrases from the book and labels for who will live where, and to populate their picture with seals separated out into the correct groups as described.

## Differentiation
**Support:** Provide children with a list of the nouns at the centre of the noun phrases to aid their search: smooth-worn rock, hard sand, rollers, grass, sand-dunes, islands, deep water.

**Extension:** Challenge children to write a short passage under their picture, explaining its importance to Kotick and the seal colony.

## 7. Brave mongoose!

### Objective

To identify how language, structure and presentation contribute to meaning.

### What you need

Copies of *The Jungle Book*; examples of age-appropriate graphic novels; images of a black cobra, mongoose, muskrat, tailor-bird, brown snake, coppersmith barbet.

### Cross-curricular link

Science

### What to do

- Remind children that Rikki-tikki-tavi is the superhero of the story in Chapter 5. Together, recap on the events in the story in order, encouraging the children to use the book for reference: 1. Rikki-tikki is washed away. 2. He is rescued. 3. He meets Nag, Nagaina and the other animals. 4. Teddy comes into the garden. 5. Rikki-tikki kills Karait. 6. He meets Chuchundra. 7. He kills Nag. 8. He destroys the eggs. 9. Nagaina threatens Teddy. 10. Rikki-tikki shows Nagaina the egg. 11. Rikki kills Nagaina.

- Explain that superhero Rikki needs his own graphic novel of his adventure. Share a range of age-appropriate graphic novels. Make a list of their features. Locate fronted adverbials such as 'Meanwhile' and other cohesive devices.

- Ask the children, in pairs, to go through the story of Rikki-tikki-tavi, noting down the key details and any associated descriptions and direct speech.

- Look at images of the animals from the story, leaving them displayed for reference.

- Ask the children to write their graphic novel of 'Rikki-Tikki-Tavi'.

### Differentiation

**Support:** Encourage children to focus on three scenes: killing Nag, showing Nagaina the egg, following Nagaina into the hole.

**Extension:** Challenge children to create a detailed and dramatic graphic version of the story, complete with cohesive devices.

## 8. Tell me more

### Objectives

To use relative clauses beginning with 'who', 'which', 'where', 'when', 'that' or with an implied relative pronoun.

### What you need

Photocopiable page 31 'Tell me more'; copies of *The Jungle Book*.

### What to do

- Ask the children to locate the relative clause in the following sentence: 'Shere Khan, who had just eaten a pig, slept in the ravine.' Ask: *What word does the relative clause start with?* ('who') Ask: *Which other words can a relative clause start with?* ('that', 'which', 'where', 'when', 'whose') Discuss how some sentences have an implied relative pronoun (where the actual word is missed out). For example, 'The bull (that) Mowgli rode was called Rama'.

- Ask the children to work with a partner to add a relative clause to this sentence, and hold it up on a whiteboard: 'The camel said he had fought a white monster.' (For example 'which was really a tent he had knocked over'.)

- Hand out photocopiable page 31 'Tell me more' and ask the children to complete the page.

- Share the children's clauses and discuss the extra information given, particularly if it refers to motive or feelings, for example: 'Mowgli, who was delighted to be in charge at last, made it clear to the children that he was the master.'

### Differentiation

**Support:** Provide children with further examples in which to locate the relative clause before attempting the activity. If helpful, provide the children with a series of relative clauses to match to the sentences.

**Extension:** Encourage children to write extended relative clauses that provide information on motive or feelings. Ask them to write their own complete sentences.

# Shadow puppets

- Stick these characters onto card and cut them out.
- Mount them on craft sticks.

Mother wolf

Father wolf

Baby Mowgli

Tabaqui

Shere Khan

Akela

Bagheera

Baloo

# Battle of the cats

● Describe Shere Khan and Bagheera. Choose your vocabulary carefully.

**Shere Khan**

**Key characteristics**

* _____
_____

* _____
_____

* _____
_____

_____
_____
_____

**Bagheera**

**Key characteristics**

* _____
_____

* _____
_____

* _____
_____

_____
_____
_____

# Tell me more

- Add a relative clause (beginning 'who', 'which', 'where', 'when', 'whose', 'that') to each sentence to add more detail. You can put the clause in the middle or at the end of the sentence.

- Note: remember to use a comma or a pair of commas!

**1.** Mowgli held up the red flower.

_____

_____

_____

**2.** Mowgli was gone and Baloo roared with sorrow.

_____

_____

_____

**3.** Mowgli made it clear to the children that he was the master.

_____

_____

_____

**4.** The villagers cast Mowgli out.

_____

_____

_____

**5.** Kotick searched for the Sea Vitch.

_____

_____

_____

# TALK ABOUT IT ▶

## 1. The Law of the Jungle

### Objective
To prepare poems to read aloud.

### What you need
Copies of *The Jungle Book*, photocopiable page 35 'The Law of the Jungle'.

### Cross-curricular link
Citizenship

### What to do

- Re-read the sections that include the two wolf council meetings in Chapter 1. Agree that the wolves live by strict laws that govern how they behave towards each other. Recap on any previous discussions you've had about the theme of 'The Law of the Jungle' in *The Jungle Book*.

- Hand out photocopiable page 35 'The Law of the Jungle', a poem which comes from *The Second Jungle Book*, also by Rudyard Kipling.

- Read the poem together, explaining any lines that the children don't understand.

- Organise the children into groups and ask each group to prepare the poem for performance. Encourage them to think creatively about their performance. For example, they could take two lines each to learn off by heart and recite in order, while the rest of the group create a mime to accompany the poem; create a slide-show showing photographs of wolves and matching the lines in the poem, as they recite; learn the whole poem as a group to recite together.

### Differentiation
**Extension:** Challenge children to learn larger amounts of the poem (the whole poem is out of copyright and easily available).

## 2. The strength of the pack

### Objective
To participate actively in collaborative conversations, staying on topic and initiating and responding to comments.

### What you need
Copies of *The Jungle Book*; photocopiable page 35 'The Law of the Jungle'.

### Cross-curricular link
Citizenship

### What to do

- Revisit the poem 'The Law of the Jungle' on photocopiable page 35, handing out individual copies. Focus on the line 'For the strength of the Pack is the Wolf, and the strength of the Wolf is the Pack.' Ask: *What do you think this means?* (For example: 'The wolf is strong because he is part of a team; the pack is strong because the wolves work together.')

- Organise the children into discussion groups and give each group copies of *The Jungle Book* and a whiteboard to make notes on.

- Ask the children, in their groups, to find examples of where the story of Mowgli supports the quotation above. (Suggest they look at both council meetings and the scene where the wolves and Mowgli work together to defeat Shere Khan at the ravine.) Remind the children about the rules of a group discussion: listening to each other, building on each other's ideas, making sure all comments are on topic, ensuring that everyone in the group is talking a similar amount (no one too much or too little).

### Differentiation
**Support:** Provide children with a list of events to discuss.

**Extension:** Challenge children to discuss what the strength of man is in this story.

# 3. Man versus beast

## Objective

To participate in discussions; to ask relevant questions to extend their understanding and knowledge.

## What you need

Copies of *The Jungle Book*.

## Cross-curricular link

Citizenship

## What to do

- Before beginning this activity, you will need to decide if this is a suitable discussion for your class.

- Some people have accused Kipling of being racist and patronising towards the native Indians in *The Jungle Book*. Others disagree and see Kipling as only setting his book within the world he knew. Provide the children with a simple summary of the situation in India at the end of the 19th century, explaining how Britain ruled India as part of the British Empire. Discuss how Kipling's writing was influenced by his time living in India.

- Ask the children, in groups, to discuss: *How does Kipling show humans in the story?* (Point them towards Chapters 3, 4, 6 and 7.) (The humans can be quite violent towards animals, powerful and superstitious in places.)

- Bring the class together to share their responses.

- Then explore together some of the problematic issues such as Kipling's portrayal of the Indians and the white men. Ask: *Does Kipling treat white men better than the Indians in the stories? What do the Indians think of the white people? Does Kipling think animals are better than people?* Encourage children to ask their own questions and together discuss possible answers.

## Differentiation

**Support:** Ask children to focus on why humans are stronger than animals in the book.

**Extension:** Challenge children to find out more about the British Raj before carrying out this activity.

# 4. Themes and ideas

## Objectives

To identify and discuss themes.

## What you need

Copies of *The Jungle Book*, photocopiable page 36 'Jungle Book themes'.

## What to do

- Ask: *What are the main ideas in* The Jungle Book? Discuss different ideas, encouraging the children to use examples from the text.

- Hand out photocopiable page 36 'Jungle Book themes' and discuss each theme in turn briefly. (Law of the animals: wolf society, monkey society; Baloo's lessons; seal colony; order of the troops in 'Servants of the Queen'. Family: Mowgli's wolf family, Mowgli's human family; the family bond between the elephants; Rikki-tikki-tavi's family; Kotick's huge family. Loyalty: the wolves' loyalty (or not) to Akela and to Mowgli; Mowgli's loyalty with Bagheera and Baloo; Rikki-tikki-tavi's loyalty towards his family. Rebel children: Mowgli; Kotick; Toomai. Man versus animals: Mowgli as man or wolf; Mowgli and the fire; Petersen catching elephants; men killing seals; animals discussing fighting with or for masters in last story.)

- Ask the children in groups to discuss each theme further, making notes on the photocopiable sheet. Encourage them to talk about where in the book the themes are demonstrated; and which characters are involved and how.

- Assign each group a theme to champion in a class debate, taking turns to argue why their theme is the most important. Then have a class vote on the most important theme.

## Differentiation

**Support:** Provide children with event cards to discuss and stick down against each theme.

**Extension:** Challenge children to create a persuasive speech in favour of their theme, using some of Akela's rhetorical techniques such as repetition and lists of three.

## 5. Missing scenes

**Objective**

To participate in role play [and] improvisations.

**What you need**

Copies of *The Jungle Book*, photocopiable page 37 'Missing scenes'.

**What to do**

- Explain that there are some events in Mowgli's story that we only hear reports of and that you are going to look at two of these together. Hand out photocopiable page 37 'Missing scenes'. Read each scenario with the class ('Mowgli's Brothers' from 'I hunt among the ploughed fields…' to '… that ye come one by one.'; 'Kaa's Hunting' from 'Mowgli had been trying to make himself heard…' to 'I will play with them again'), clarifying when they would have taken place.

- Share together the clues in the text that suggest what has happened (the things Mowgli can hear in the distance, Akela's report of the plot to trick him; Mowgli's account of meeting the monkeys and what they said and did).

- Organise the children, in small groups, to choose one of the scenarios to role play.
  *Wolves against Akela:* Encourage the children to bring out how Shere Khan flatters and manipulates the wolves. Help them to find the parts of the text that explain the missed kill.
  *Mowgli and the Monkey People:* Encourage the children to bring out how silly and untrustworthy the monkeys are. Ask them to imagine how Mowgli feels when he has been beaten by Baloo.
- Share the role plays. Pause after each role play to hot-seat one of the characters.

**Differentiation**

**Support:** Encourage children to write notes about what they want to say in their role play before they begin.

**Extension:** Challenge children to think deeply about the characters' motivation.

## 6. Film of the book

**Objective**

To give well-structured descriptions, explanations and narratives for different purposes, including for expressing feelings.

**What you need**

DVD of *The Jungle Book* (Disney, 2016) or *The Jungle Book* (Disney, 1967), copies of *The Jungle Book*.

**What to do**

- Watch one of the two Disney films of *The Jungle Book*. The 1967 version is a comic cartoon musical (which includes the Beatles as four vultures); the 2016 version is a sumptuous live-action film with impressive CGI.

- Afterwards, discuss how the children feel about the film. Organise the children into discussion groups, each with copies of the book to refer to, and ask them to discuss: *How was the film the same as the book?* Ask the children to think about plot and character. *How was the film different from the book?* Again, think about plot and character. *Which did you like best: the book or the film?* Encourage them to explain why.

- Ask the groups to note down their thoughts about the film, organising them under headings. Groups then present their thoughts to the class, describing the film and their different responses to it.

- If possible, over a longer period of time, watch and compare both films and have a vote on which the children prefer, discussing which is closer to the book.

**Differentiation**

**Extension:** Challenge children to discuss whether the idea in the song 'Look for the bare necessities' fits with the 'Law of the Jungle'.

# The Law of the Jungle

*NOW this is the Law of the Jungle*
*— as old and as true as the sky;*
*And the Wolf that shall keep it may prosper,*
*but the Wolf that shall break it must die.*

*As the creeper that girdles the tree-trunk*
*the Law runneth forward and back —*
*For the strength of the Pack is the Wolf,*
*and the strength of the Wolf is the Pack.*

Wash daily from nose-tip to tail-tip;
drink deeply, but never too deep;
And remember the night is for hunting,
and forget not the day is for sleep.

The Jackal may follow the Tiger,
but, Cub, when thy whiskers are grown,
Remember the Wolf is a Hunter
— go forth and get food of thine own.

Keep peace with the Lords of the Jungle
— the Tiger, the Panther, and Bear.
And trouble not Hathi the Silent,
and mock not the Boar in his lair.

When Pack meets with Pack in the Jungle,
and neither will go from the trail,
Lie down till the leaders have spoken
— it may be fair words shall prevail…

*Now these are the Laws of the Jungle,*
*and many and mighty are they;*
*But the head and the hoof of the Law*
*and the haunch and the hump is — Obey!*

Rudyard Kipling

# Jungle Book themes

- Which of these themes is the most important? Discuss each in turn.

- Note down any events in *The Jungle Book* that fit with the theme.

| Theme | Notes |
|---|---|
| Law of the animals | |
| Family | |
| Loyalty | |
| Rebel children | |
| Man versus animals | |

# Missing scenes

- Discuss what might happen in each of these scenes. Read the passage suggested and think about the questions asked.

- Choose one scene to role play in your group.

## Scene 1. Wolves against Akela

Shere Khan and the wolves who admire him discuss how to remove Akela from power. Perhaps the wolves tell Shere Khan that he can have Mowgli once they are in control of the Pack.

**Read:** 'Mowgli's brothers' – Read the passage where Mowgli hears Akela missing the kill and the opening of the second meeting at the Council Rock where Akela explains that the missed kill was a trick by the rebel wolves.

**Characters:** Shere Khan, Tabaqui, rebel wolves

**Think:**

- What does Shere Khan want?

- What does Shere Khan think about the wolves?

- What do the rebel wolves want?

- What do they think about Shere Khan?

- What do the rebel wolves think about Akela?

## Scene 2. Mowgli and the Monkey People

The Monkey People find Mowgli in the jungle. They tell him that they want him to be their leader and describe how they will swing through the branches all day and throw mud at Baloo.

**Read:** 'Kaa's Hunting' – Read the conversation between Mowgli and Baloo where Mowgli tells Baloo that he has met the monkeys and Baloo warns Mowgli about them.

**Characters:** Mowgli, different monkeys, perhaps Bagheera is watching.

**Think:**

- What do the monkeys want?

- Will the monkeys let Mowgli be their leader?

- What does Mowgli like about the monkeys?

- What does Mowgli feel about Baloo at the beginning of the scene?

# GET WRITING ▶

## 1. Raised by wolves

> **Objective**
>
> To select the appropriate form and use other similar writing as models for their own.
>
> **What you need**
>
> Copies of *The Jungle Book*, example newspapers at the right level, photocopiable page 41 'Human child raised by wolves'.

**What to do**

- Ask the children to imagine that they are a newspaper reporter commissioned to write a report about Mowgli. In preparation for that, ask them to carry out a role play.

- In groups ask the children to choose roles: reporter (with clipboard), Mowgli, Messua, Buldeo and other villagers. Tell them to decide whether Mowgli has recently arrived in the village or just been sent away after killing Shere Khan. Ask them to carry out their role play in which the reporter talks to the villagers and takes notes. Encourage them to think what the villagers might say, for example, Messua: 'I knew at once that he was my son' and Buldeo: 'The boy is a sorcerer and a liar!'

- After the role play, look at newspaper reports at the right reading level and ask the children to help you draw up a newspaper features list.

- Hand out photocopiable page 41 'Human child raised by wolves', and ask the children to plan and then write their newspaper report.

- Encourage them to use the checklist and partner feedback to improve their report.

> **Differentiation**
>
> **Extension:** Challenge children to capture a range of opinions about Mowgli.

## 2. What did you think?

> **Objectives**
>
> To select appropriate grammar and vocabulary, understanding how such choices can change and enhance meaning.
>
> **What you need**
>
> DVD of *The Jungle Book* (Disney 2016) or *The Jungle Book* (Disney 1967).

**What to do**

- If you have not already done so, watch one of the excellent Disney films of *The Jungle Book*.

- Ask the children in pairs to role play telling someone (who hasn't seen it) all about it. Tell them to swap roles and ask questions.

- Discuss the information they shared in their role play: plot (but not the ending), style, whether it was funny, sad, exciting, favourite scene and so on. Ask: *What sort of language did you use?* Capture the vocabulary and suggest additional words that might be useful ('enchanting', 'hilarious', 'terrifying', 'spectacular', 'mesmerising' and so on).

- Share a model review of an age-appropriate film. Look at the different information provided: title, studio, date, length, certificate, main actors, number of stars given and the text about the film.

- Ask the children to write a review of a film of *The Jungle Book*.

- Once they've finished a first draft, encourage them to improve their vocabulary and spelling. Encourage them to write a final draft that uses different text sizes and an illustration.

> **Differentiation**
>
> **Support:** Provide children with a template to work with.
>
> ---
>
> **Extension:** Challenge them to write paired reviews showing how the vocabulary can change the meaning.

# 3. Cut it out!

## Objective
To draft and write by précising longer passages.

## What you need
Photocopiable page 42 'Lazy jungle life'.

## What to do

- Provide individuals with photocopiable page 42 'Lazy jungle life' and read the extract together, discussing the time that Kipling takes to build up a detailed picture.

- Challenge the children to list the things Mowgli has learned, the different sounds in the passage, the different animals mentioned, and the different verbs.

- Once you have finished admiring Kipling's skill in creating a beautifully slow and lazy description of many years, explain that we want to get on with the story more quickly and don't have time for this indulgence.

- Explain to the children that the passage is 283 words and you want to cut it down to 100 words. Tell them to first cross out words that aren't necessary (for example anything in brackets, extra description and so on). Next tell them to start rewriting the passage, paraphrasing where necessary but attempting to retain as much of Kipling's original vocabulary as possible.

- Share the new texts. Discuss what has been lost (atmosphere, style) and what has been gained (perhaps it's easier to understand, or more dramatic).

## Differentiation

**Support:** Provide children with a shorter passage to work with by creating a version of the photocopiable page that finishes at 'business man'. Ask them to cut it down to around 90 words.

**Extension:** Challenge children to ensure that their précis still has an elegance about it. Encourage them to retain some of the repetition used in the original.

# 4. Tiger in danger!

## Objectives
To use organisational and presentational devices to structure the text and guide the reader.

## What you need
Large paper and craft materials; photographs of tigers; access to the internet; list of safe websites to visit.

## Cross-curricular link
Science

## What to do

- Ask the children to tell you about Shere Khan. List a range of adjectives: 'cunning', 'mean', 'hungry', 'lame', 'calculating', 'obsessed' and so on.

- Display an image of a beautiful Bengal tiger. Explain that Shere Khan's descendants in India are endangered.

- Organise the children with books and internet access (to previously checked sites, such as National Geographic Kids, World Wildlife Fund and so on) to research the plight of the Bengal tiger. Ask them to make notes about the tiger: where it lives, how big it is, how fast it runs, what it eats, how many there are, why it is under threat.

- Look together at examples of information posters (perhaps around the school or on the internet) and identify some key features (large heading, images, facts, attractive design, descriptive language).

- Ask the children to create a poster about the Bengal tiger, using short paragraphs of text, a main image, facts and a bulleted list. Suggest to the children that they combine information about the tiger with facts about the problems it is facing.

## Differentiation

**Support:** Encourage children to create a simple poster comprising a picture and six facts.

**Extension:** Challenge children to use persuasive and emotive language to encourage people to save the tiger.

## 5. But that's another story...

### Objective
In writing narratives, to consider how authors have developed characters and settings in what they have read.

### What you need
Copies of *The Jungle Book*, photocopiable page 43 'Jungle Book – my sequel' (to support less confident learners).

### Cross-curricular link
Geography

### What to do
- Ask the children, in groups, to discuss what could happen next in next in each of the short stories in *The Jungle Book*.

- Share the ideas, until the board is full of new scenarios for the characters, for example: a new tiger threatens Mowgli; hunters, or scientists, or tourists come to Kotick's new home; Kotick has a baby who goes missing; a dog arrives in Rikki-tikki-tavi's house and only Rikki knows he's nasty; Toomai frees all the elephants; a village is attacked and the 'Servants of the Queen' go into battle together to help; Two Tails becomes brave; Hathi, the elephant, is captured by Petersen but Mowgli and Toomai rescue him.

- Tell the children to plan a sequel to one of the stories using any of the ideas from the board.

- Encourage them to return to *The Jungle Book* to remember character and setting. Tell them to note down details on their plan, building on what they know.

- Ask the children to write – or storyboard – their new story.

### Differentiation
**Support:** Provide children with photocopiable page 43 'Jungle Book – my sequel' to support them as they plan a sequel for Mowgli.

**Extension:** Challenge children to develop one of the themes from *The Jungle Book* in their writing.

## 6. The Song of the Jungle

### Objective
To perform their own compositions, using appropriate intonation, volume and movement so that meaning is clear.

### What you need
Copies of *The Jungle Book*.

### Cross-curricular link
Music

### What to do
- Divide the class in two and ask one side to be the first speaker and one side to be the second, then read together the poem at the beginning of Chapter 3 'Tiger! Tiger!'

- Ask the children to write their own question and answer poem about Mowgli in the jungle. Discuss ideas: honey, lying in trees, swinging with the monkeys, swimming and so on. For example: 'What of the honey so sticky and sweet? *Brother, it's hard to reach but good to eat.* What of the monkeys? Please tell me do. *Brother, we taught them a lesson or two.*' Tell the children that their poems do not need to rhyme.

- If useful, provide them with the text on photocopiable page 42 'Lazy jungle life' to help with ideas.

- Encourage the children to draft and redraft their poem, and to share their work with a partner to help them improve it.

- Once the children are happy with their poems, tell them to practice a performance. Encourage brave and musical children to write a tune for the poem, or to create a rhythm with blocks or cymbals.

- Share poems as a class.

### Differentiation
**Support:** Ask children to work in a group to create a shared poem.

**Extension:** Challenge children to create a poem that rhymes and scans.

# Human child raised by wolves

- Use this chart to make notes for your newspaper report.
- When you've finished your first draft, use the checklist to make sure you have included everything.

**Headline:** _____

**Introductory sentence (who, what, where, when):**

_____

**Explain more about the story:**




**Quotation from head-man:**

_____

_____

**Quotation from Buldeo:**

_____

_____

**Quotation from Messua:**

_____

_____

**Image:**




**Caption:**

**Checklist:** ☐ Headline  ☐ Opening sentence  ☐ Story explained
☐ Quotation  ☐ Image  ☐ Caption

# Lazy jungle life

Now you must be content to skip ten or eleven whole years, and only guess at all the wonderful life that Mowgli led among the wolves, because if it were written out it would fill ever so many books. He grew up with the cubs, though they, of course, were grown wolves almost before he was a child, and Father Wolf taught him his business, and the meaning of things in the jungle, till every rustle in the grass, every breath of the warm night air, every note of the owls above his head, every scratch of a bat's claws as it roosted for a while in a tree, and every splash of every little fish jumping in a pool meant just as much to him as the work of his office means to a business man. When he was not learning he sat out in the sun and slept, and ate, and went to sleep again; when he felt dirty or hot he swam in the forest pools; and when he wanted honey (Baloo told him that honey and nuts were just as pleasant to eat as raw meat) he climbed up for it, and that Bagheera showed him how to do.

Bagheera would lie out on a branch and call, "Come along, Little Brother," and at first Mowgli would cling like the sloth, but afterwards he would fling himself through the branches almost as boldly as the grey ape. He took his place at the Council Rock, too, when the Pack met, and there he discovered that if he stared hard at any wolf, the wolf would be forced to drop his eyes, and so he used to stare for fun.

# Jungle Book – my sequel

● The story of Mowgli ends with Mowgli and four cubs leaving the pack to live alone. What happens next? Plan an adventure for Mowgli and the cubs.

**Characters:** Who will be in the story: characters from *The Jungle Book* and/ or new characters?

_____

_____

_____

_____

_____

**Setting:** Which setting will you describe? Note some noun phrases here.

_____

_____

_____

_____

_____

**Beginning:** What trigger begins the adventure? Who or what arrives?

_____

_____

_____

**Middle:** How does the story develop? Are there more problems? Do more characters arrive?

_____

_____

_____

_____

**End:** How is the story resolved?

_____

_____

_____

# ASSESSMENT ▶

## 1. Theme jungle

### Objectives
To identify and discuss themes and conventions.

### What you need
Copies of *The Jungle Book*, large pieces of paper, photocopiable page 36 'Jungle Book themes'.

### What to do

- Remind the children of the previous discussion and work on the themes in *The Jungle Book*.

- Ask the children to draw a theme jungle for *The Jungle Book*. Ask them to draw the simple outline of three rainforest-style trees (with the heads at different heights to make the best use of the space), leaving space for a fourth tree to be added later. Ask them to write a different theme along the length of each trunk (choosing from the list of 'Jungle Book themes' on photocopiable page 36). Tell them to write events and relationships that fit with the theme along the branches and within the outline of the rest of the tree, perhaps using a different branch for each story or aspect. Allow them to use the book for reference.

- Move on to discuss the world of *The Jungle Book*. Ask: *How is this world different from ours?* (animals talk, have meetings, have friendships between species, have plans and rules of behaviour, don't always eat each other) Ask the children to draw a fourth tree and write the words 'Jungle world' along the trunk. Ask them to fill the tree with all the ways that the world of *The Jungle Book* is different from ours.

### Differentiation
**Support:** Ask children to choose one theme and draw a tree for it.

**Extension:** Challenge children to cover elements from all seven stories in their theme jungle.

## 2. Character match

### Objective
To discuss and evaluate how authors use language, including figurative language, considering the impact on the reader.

### What you need
Copies of *The Jungle Book*, photocopiable page 47 'Character match'.

### What to do

- Hand out photocopiable page 47 'Character match' to children working in pairs. Ask the children to cut out the quotations and match them to the characters they describe.

- Share the answers to ensure that the children have matched the characters to the correct phrases. Then ask the children to stick each quotation into the correct box.

- Ask children to add to each box one thing that they remember about the character – something they did, something they said or something someone said about them. Encourage the children to attempt to write their statement without checking in the book, but allow them to find an example in the book if they become stuck.

- Finally, ask them to write their own description of the character. Suggest they use Kipling's technique of a long list.

- Share the descriptions with the class, challenging the rest of the class to guess the character described.

### Differentiation
**Support:** Ask children to focus on matching the quotation to the character and writing one thing they remember about the character.

# 3. Why did you do that?

## Objective

To draw inferences such as inferring characters' motives from their actions, and to justify inferences with evidence.

## What you need

Copies of *The Jungle Book*.

## What to do

- Write the following questions on the board:
  1. *Why does Bagheera speak up for Mowgli? What does he want?*
  2. *Why does Shere Khan flatter and encourage the younger wolves?*
  3. *Why does Kaa help Bagheera and Baloo find Mowgli?*
  4. *Why do the Jungle People hate the Monkey People?*
  5. *Why does Rikki-tikki-tavi risk everything to protect the humans?*
  6. *Why does Kala Nag take Toomai to see the elephant-dance?*

- Encourage the children to discuss each question in pairs. Ask them to think about what the character says and what he does, in order to infer motive.

- Ask the children to work individually to write an answer for each question in the format: 'I think… because…' To encourage them to think deeper, tell the children to write a second sentence for each answer. For example: 'Bagheera is interested in keeping Mowgli safe because he wants to protect him from Shere Khan. He also knows Mowgli would be a good ally to have; I think this because Bagheera teaches Mowgli to use fire'.

## Differentiation

**Support:** Allow children to focus on the first three questions. Direct them to the pages in the books where they will find the answer and encourage them to find clues about motivation from actions in the relevant passages.

**Extension:** Encourage children to write a three-sentence answer to encourage them to pull in evidence and further thought.

# 4. What next for Mowgli?

## Objective

To predict what might happen from details stated and implied.

## What you need

Copies of *The Jungle Book*.

## What to do

- Ask: *What is the situation at the end of Mowgli's story?* (He has killed Shere Khan and proved himself a man. The wolf pack remains leaderless but Mowgli has become leader of a pack of wolves, Bagheera and Baloo. We know that he will get married later on. The rebel wolves want Akela to be their leader again but he has refused, saying they will rise up again.)

- Ask the children to think about the characters in the story and what they know about them. Ask: *What dangers or power struggles still exist in the jungle?*

- Ask the children to write down three events that they think could happen if the story continued. Encourage them to explain each event in a couple of sentences and then state why they think this will happen. For example: 'Mowgli, distracted by his new life and power, forgets to give Kaa a goat. Kaa decides to attack Mowgli and Mowgli must appease him. I think this because Mowgli can be vain and impulsive – living in the moment – and would easily forget Kaa who has previously said that he might kill Mowgli.'

## Differentiation

**Support:** Provide children with a series of options to discuss and put in order of likelihood.

**Extension:** Encourage extended and well thought-through, detailed answers.

# 5. It's a classic

## Objectives
To increase familiarity with a wide range of books, including fiction from our literary heritage.

## What you need
Copies of *The Jungle Book*.

## What to do

- Organise the children into book groups and ask them to discuss their final thoughts on *The Jungle Book*. Suggest they ask each other the following questions, as a starting point: *Did you enjoy the book? Would you recommend it to a friend? What was your favourite scene? Who was your favourite character? Which story, apart from the story of Mowgli, was your favourite?*

- Afterwards, quiz children about what other people in their group thought.

- Ask the children to look back at their film review, or any other reviews that they have written. Recap on the features of a book review (details of the book's publication, author information, summary of the first part of the book, description of key strengths, emotional language) using examples from *The Jungle Book*. Explain that a review of *The Jungle Book* will need to refer to all the stories at least collectively, and one or two of the non-Mowgli stories explicitly.

- Ask the children to write a review of *The Jungle Book*, remembering to include a heading, publication details and an introduction before the main review.

## Differentiation
**Support:** Ask children to focus their review on the first three chapters.

**Extension:** Challenge children to write a comprehensive review of the entire book, mentioning all the stories and pulling them together by discussing themes across the whole book.

# 6. An emotional rollercoaster

## Objective
To use expanded noun phrases; to draw inferences such as inferring characters' feelings and to justify inferences with evidence.

## What you need
Copies of *The Jungle Book*.

## What to do

- Remind children of the final story 'Servants of the Queen' and where it is set. Write 'field' on the board and ask: *What type of word is this?* (noun) Explain that you want to make this into a more interesting noun phrase about the setting and ask for suggestions for words (determiner and adjectives) that could be added. Together, create some examples ('the muddy, wet, miserable field', 'a muddy, dark field near the Artillery lines with stacks of cannons')

- List the following settings on the board: Mother and Father Wolf's cave, the Council Rock, the jungle, the Cold Lairs, the village, the ravine, Kotick's secret home, the garden in 'Rikki-tikki-tavi', the clearing of the elephant-dance, the hill above the army camp.

- Ask the children to choose five settings from the list (encouraging them to choose at least one of the last three settings).

- For each setting, ask the children to write: the name of the setting, the key events that took place in the setting, an expanded noun phrase for the setting, a description of the emotions the main character feels in this setting and why they feel this.

## Differentiation
**Support:** Ask children to choose two settings with a partner and discuss the setting first before writing their answers.

**Extension:** Encourage children to complete as many settings as they can. Challenge them to write long, extended noun phrases and write more complicated answers about feelings.

# Character match

- Cut out the quotations and match each one to the character it is describing. Then complete the table for each character and stick each one in your book.

✂

"his hair was full of leaves... but he tried to salute"

"he eats only nuts and roots and honey"

"a voice as soft as wild honey dripping from a tree"

## Bagheera

| Quotation | |
| --- | --- |
| I remember | |
| Description | |

## Toomai

| Quotation | |
| --- | --- |
| I remember | |
| Description | |

## Baloo

| Quotation | |
| --- | --- |
| I remember | |
| Description | |

# SCHOLASTIC
# READ & RESPOND

# Available in this series:

## Key Stage 1

978-1407-18254-4

978-1407-16053-5

978-1407-14220-3

978-1407-15875-4

978-1407-16058-0

## Key Stage 2

978-1407-14228-9

978-1407-14224-1

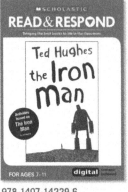

978-1407-14229-6

978-14071-6057-3

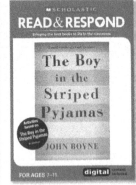

978-14071-6071-9

978-14071-6069-6

978-14071-6067-2

978-14071-4231-9

978-14071-4223-4

978-14071-6060-3

978-14071-5876-1

978-14071-6068-9

978-14071-6063-4

978-1407-18253-7

978-1407-18252-0

## To find out more, call 0845 6039091
## or visit our website www.scholastic.co.uk/readandrespond